Praise for Nicole Faires's *The Ultimate Guide to Homesteading*

"The kind of book any homesteader or wannabe homesteader should have on their shelf." —*Progressive Pioneer*

"In a word . . . 'Wow!'" —*Small Town Living*

"A compendium of skills for self-sufficiency and survival, this book contains answers to just about every practical question you might have about homesteading." —Sierra Club's *The Green Life*

"It REALLY is the ULTIMATE guide." —*The Renegade Farmer*

"Shows you how to do everything yourself, and I mean everything." —*Frugal Flora*

"Highly recommend[ed] . . . if you are interested in sustainable and independent living." —Healthy Homesteading

"A must for any person interested in living self-sustainably." —*Finger Lakes Foodie*

"Once you have this book, you will be referring to it over and over again throughout the years." —Off-Grid.net

Praise for Nicole Faires's *The Ultimate Guide to Permaculture*

"There is a lot of powerful information here for anyone on a homesteading quest, whether they are working with 1/4-acre of 140 acres." —*No Ordinary Homestead*

"The perfect book to read before developing your property into a sustainable, food-producing haven." —*Advanced Survival Guide*

Other books by Nicole Faires

The Ultimate Guide to Homesteading (2011)
The Ultimate Guide to Permaculture (2012)

FOOD
TYRANTS

FOOD TYRANTS

Fight for Your Basic Right to Healthy
Food in a Toxic World

Nicole Faires

Skyhorse Publishing

Skyhorse Publishing books may be purchased in bulk at special discounts for sales promotion, corporate gifts, fund-raising, or educational purposes. Special editions can also be created to specifications. For details, contact the Special Sales Department, Skyhorse Publishing, 307 West 36th Street, 11th Floor, New York, NY 10018 or info@skyhorsepublishing.com

Skyhorse® and Skyhorse Publishing® are registered trademarks of Skyhorse Publishing, Inc.®, a Delaware corporation.

www.skyhorsepublishing.com

10 9 8 7 6 5 4 3 2 1

Library of Congress Cataloging-in-Publication Data available on file.

ISBN: 978-1-61608-865-1

Printed in the United States of America

Table of Contents

Introduction

"We must rapidly begin the shift from a thing-oriented society to a person-oriented society. When machines and computers, profit motives and property rights are considered more important than people, the giant triplets of racism, militarism and economic exploitation are incapable of being conquered. A nation can flounder as readily in the face of moral and spiritual bankruptcy as it can through financial bankruptcy."
—Dr. Martin Luther King, April 1967

Years ago I watched an episode of *Wife Swap* that featured a particularly memorable character. The premise of the reality show is that two mothers swapped families for two weeks—and these families were far from the traditional American family. This particular woman believed that she could draw energy from the sun. Every morning she would go outside and greet the desert sunrise by staring straight into it for hours at a time, basking in its golden glow. She had forbidden her family any cooked food and had removed the stove from the house so she could become disciplined enough to subsist only on the sun's rays, her ultimate goal.

This woman became infamous because everyone knows you have to eat to live. There's no getting around it. You're not a plant—you can't stick your feet into the soil and raise your arms to the sky and expect anything other than a slow and uncomfortable death.

But no matter how crazy we might think this unfortunate sun woman may be, she is no crazier than the majority of people living in most industrialized nations. We are just as guilty in our beliefs and it would be hypocritical to laugh at her. We believe that we can eat processed foods and still receive the nutrients that we need. We have allowed our entire food system to be hijacked by corporations. Is that any better than trying to absorb our nourishment from the sun?

Trying to absorb nutrients from foods processed and packed in factories is killing us, gradually but undeniably. In North America, we have become increasingly aware of the problem because of popular documentaries like *Forks Over Knives* and *Food, Inc.* But now that we know, we find that it's very difficult to take control of our food because we've already given up our right to do so. Government legislation both federally and locally has taken away our freedom to produce it and eat it; the suburbs have taken over the farms and the farmers are gone; and the food we do get might as well just be labeled with a big stamp that says Cancer.

But you know all of this. You already know about the health effects of processed food, and you are already aware that your food supply is in trouble, otherwise you would be reading some other book. Be warned that this book recommends *subversion*. Rebellion. This book advocates growing your own food no matter what. If you choose to do something that your government considers illegal, I take no responsibility for that.

I just don't think you have much of a choice.

CHAPTER ONE

The Foundation of Food

"I saw all the people hustling early in the morning to go into the factories and stores and the office buildings, to do their job, to get their check. But ultimately it's not office buildings or jobs that give us our checks. It's the soil. The soil is what gives us the real income that supports us all."

—Ed Begley, Jr.

The Abridgement of Freedom

"I believe there are more instances of the abridgement of freedom of the people by gradual and silent encroachments by those in power than by violent and sudden usurpations."

—James Madison

You may not realize it yet, but you do not have the legal right to grow and eat anything that you want, and food has become a very complex issue. However, this right was not lost overnight, because originally food was not political. Article 1, Section 8 of the US Constitution would have included agriculture if any of the founding members or later leaders believed that the government had any say in the matter. Our relatively young food "industry" was still safe in the 1920s, when President Coolidge vetoed a complex price-fixing bill for various crops. He said, "I do not believe that upon serious consideration the farmers of America would tolerate the precedent of a

1

body of men chosen solely by one industry who, acting in the name of the Government, shall arrange for contracts which determine prices. . . . Such action would establish bureaucracy on such a scale as to dominate not only the economic life but the moral, social, and political future of our people."

This bureaucracy he meant to avoid, however, is now a staple of most of the food industry legislation in America today. Only ten years after Coolidge, Hoover introduced the Farm Board, which fixed the price of wheat and cotton. The Farm Board had good intentions, but its policies had far-reaching consequences. If the price of wheat or cotton dropped too low, the government would step in and buy it at the fixed price. This relative financial security convinced many farmers to start producing wheat and cotton, and pretty soon they had too much of it. Supply far outstripped demand. That's when President Roosevelt created the Agricultural Adjustment Act. Rather than paying farmers too much for a worthless crop, the government now paid them *not* to grow wheat or cotton. By that logic, any business that got into trouble by poorly estimating the market should be "bailed out" and paid to prevent stupidity. But this only applied to farmers.

These subsidies had a completely unexpected result many years later. When corn became subsidized, farmers began overproducing it in the same way they had wheat and cotton. So, to find a market for all that extra corn, the United States began producing massive amounts of inexpensive high fructose corn syrup, which became a major ingredient in many, many manufactured foods. We're now very aware how bad high fructose corn syrup is for us, and yet the USDA, which is responsible for publishing healthy food guides for millions of children, has no problem handing out money for it.

However, to truly find a solution for our nation's food problems, it is necessary to go all the way back to the foundation of food: the soil. When we talk about the loss of our right to healthy food, what we are really talking about is losing our freedom to access soil to grow it. When we talk about the toxic state of the factory farms supplying the majority of our food supply, what we are really discussing is the gross mismanagement of our land. We are so quickly destroying our ability to feed ourselves that in a short while we will be completely dependent on others. This all comes down to dirt.

It is no longer possible to allow others to retain responsibility for our food supply without severely endangering a healthy future for the next generation. This means that the current rhetoric of *Know Your Farmer* will need to become much more personal. It should be *Everyone Is a Farmer*. I am hopeful that someday we will live in a culture where growing food is a matter of course, something almost everyone will do on balconies and backyards, and farms will dot urban landscapes on every corner, employing vast numbers of willing unemployed workers. This is the path to the restoration of our full freedoms, but it will not come without a cost. The deeply entrenched corporate agenda of the USDA, the millions of dollars corporations pour into legislation, and our own voracious appetites stand in the way.

The Loss of Farmland

"Quit thinking about decent land use as solely an economic problem. Examine each question in terms of what is ethically and esthetically right, as well as what is economically expedient. A thing is right when it tends to preserve the integrity, stability and beauty of the biotic community. It is wrong when it tends otherwise."

—Aldo Leopold

According to the American Farmland Trust, America lost farmland at a rate of one acre per minute between 2002 and 2007, totaling 4 million acres, and that rate has only increased. Urban development, suburban sprawl, and commercial building all find farmland appealing for the same reasons it is good for farming: It has been cleared and leveled and has good drainage.

Unfortunately, not all soil can grow plants. Decent farmland is actually relatively rare in comparison to the rest of the terrain. Rocky places, forests, floodplains, mountains, rivers, lakes, and canyons don't make good farmland and are more than likely not worth transforming.

Why don't farmers just stop selling their land? The number one reason is that farmers are getting old. USDA farm census numbers show that in 1997 the average farmer was fifty-four years old, and by 2007 the average had become fifty-seven. This would not be a terrible problem if more than 1 percent (as opposed to 38 percent in 1900) of the population actually farmed the land and those farmers were not aging. Most of the next generation doesn't seem interested in taking over these farms, and so the farmers sell land to finance their retirement or even medical bills. As the demand for land increases, the next generation of farmers finds itself priced out of the market by wealthy developers.

There are some who downplay the loss of farms by rationalizing that 4 million acres isn't really that much in relation to America's total landmass, which is about 2.4 billion acres. But this farmland is the most valuable acreage in America because of its soil quality. Good farmland usually has a couple of feet of precious topsoil, but the quality is not simply measured by the quantity of nutrients it has. The structure of the soil is just as important because it can take decades or even hundreds of years to build up a mixture that is perfect. Besides *humus* (decayed organic matter), there are minerals, clay, and sand that come together to retain water, but still let it drain at the right rate and insulate roots at just the right temperature. This kind of rare and valuable soil is called *loam*.

Many farms in the United States have been cultivated since they were first cleared during the Colonial period. When the settlers arrived, they found much of North America fully forested, and so they had to clear the land by hand, removing trees and rocks. The forest floor made a rich base for plant life. Some of the land lay in fertile valleys that had been flooded by rising lakes and rivers and fertilized by fish. The early farmers worked the land carefully and sustainably and never pushed the soil beyond its limits. This practice continued until the 1920s, when war and mechanization changed how farming was done. Young men came home from the front only to leave again for city jobs. They were soon replaced by tractors. Farms began to focus on *monoculture*, or growing one type of food only, rather than producing meat, vegetables, and grain together in the aesthetic form we still picture in our minds today. The size of these farms increased as investors bought up generational farmland and conglomerated it.

Underutilized chemical factories left idle after the war were put to work creating chemical fertilizer, herbicides, and fungicides. On a large scale, the historical and fertile farmland of the past became contaminated by toxic materials and depleted of any nutrients, as farmers became completely dependent on chemicals. Farmers were stunned when they began experiencing mass crop failure and tremendous soil problems on farmland that had faithfully provided for generations, but it wasn't until the catastrophic drought of the 1930s that people realized how bad the situation was. America's heartland dried up, and the overgrazed and overplowed soil simply blew away for the next eight years. According to Cary Nelson, by 1934, the drought affected 75 percent of the United States, and the billowing soil carried by the wind created horrific dust storms that killed thousands of people. Sunday, April 14, 1935, became known to history as Black Sunday, as a mountain of dust rolling across the Plains turned day into night. People were stranded for hours as the tsunami of topsoil made its way across the Midwest and travelled all the way to Washington, DC. It was because of this storm that the region became known as the Dust Bowl.

Just a few weeks before Black Sunday, President Roosevelt's advisor Hugh Hammond Bennett had testified before Congress that the nation desperately needed better soil conservation methods. When the dust obscured the sun, he pointed out the window to his colleagues and said, "This, gentlemen, is what I've been talking about." Obviously there was very little argument, and Congress created the Soil Conservation Service under the USDA before the end of that year. Farmers were taught to use crop rotation, cover crops, better plowing techniques, and basic soil care, all skills their forefathers had been using only forty years before. Nelson found that planting windbreaks and alternative plowing strategies reduced erosion by 65 percent, but by that time there had already been a massive exodus away from the Midwest as crops failed. Skeletons of farms were strewn across the Plains as farmers abandoned farming for good, leaving the land to be repossessed by banks.

In 1942, J. I. Rodale promoted the word *organic* to describe a method of farming that did not use chemicals and took care of the soil, but it was forty years before that method was embraced and any real change began. The chemical industry was (and still is) a very powerful force, and it wasn't until the 1990s that more than a few outspoken activists, scientists, and die-hard gardeners took any real notice of it. One hundred years after our departure from sustainable growing methods, farmers and consumers are finally beginning to recognize that some of the soil-conserving methods of the past are better for the soil—and for us. However, despite our awareness of the problem, and the massive drought of the 1930s, there has not been enough change. According to the National Oceanic and Atmospheric Administration (NOAA), 2012 has seen the worst drought since the Dust Bowl, affecting 56 percent of the United States with moderate to extreme drought in June. At the time of this writing, much of the soybean, wheat, and corn crop has been lost, and better soil management practices could have prevented it.

The damage has already been done. Even though the number of sustainable farms has been increasing every year, available farmland has also been shrinking at a steady rate. Considering that the vast majority of farms are not using sustainable soil practices despite the efforts of the Soil Conservation Service (now known as the NRCS), our available fertile soil is decreasing through each mismanaged crop cycle. Add to this our increasing population and dependence on cheap imported food and the rate could be even higher. The USDA census estimates the United States lost 1.7 percent of its farmland within a five-year span, which means that with all factors considered, all of America's farmland will probably be completely gone within three hundred years. That may seem like a long time, but consider the effect of losing just 20 percent of the farmland. A country so dependent on imports for food is a country that will fall victim to rising prices, substandard quality, and even possible political turmoil. Food is so vital for survival that it becomes a mechanism of control. If you don't see it, your children will within the next sixty years.

Soil 101

"If the soil is destroyed, then our liberty of action and choice are gone."
—Walter Clay Lowdermilk, 1953

What is the difference between *soil* and *dirt*? Generally, most people think dirt is a dead substance that is not capable of growing a living thing. The dust of the desert or land cleared for building a house is just dirt. They may also think that soil is the stuff you buy in bags decorated with smiling cartoon flowers or that it comes in trucks from the local supply store.

In other words, there is an idea floating around that humans make soil, and the earth makes dirt.

Nothing could be farther from the truth. Except in the case of some very big deserts, most places in the world had very fertile soil at some point. Infinite communities of bacteria and microbes create a complex layer cake of matter, gases, and liquids that is perfectly suited to the root systems of plants, and this happens all on its own when left undisturbed. It is a complex cycle that does quite well without our interference. When humans arrive on the scene and set up farming and civilization, we create dirt. Dirt is soil that has been displaced, with orphan particles missing key pieces that make it alive. We do this because we are ignorant of the microscopic life living below the surface of the ground. We destroy the soil's innate ability to regulate the flow of water, which then stops it from adequately filtering and cleaning the water, and in the process we rob it of the power to store and provide nutrients.

This, of course, creates all kinds of monumental problems. Erosion, crop loss, flooding, dust storms, dropping water tables, radon, salt buildup, and even allergies and asthma are directly related to human destruction of the soil. Dr. Walter Clay Lowdermilk was a noted soil conservationist who worked as the assistant chief of the USDA in the 1930s. He travelled extensively all over the world studying the soil, and at the end of his tour he gave a series of lectures that became a pamphlet in 1948 titled *Conquest of the Land through Seven Thousand Years.* In it he documented the causes of war, the decline of civilizations, and the destruction of society. In his opinion, it all came down to one thing: "For even you and I will sell our liberty and more for food, when driven to this tragic choice. There is no substitute for food."

And food will not grow without soil.

Soil is Alive

What we call soil is really just a container for a microcosm of living creatures, most of which we can't see. A single shovelful of soil contains more species than are found in the entire Amazon rain forest, such as these organisms:

- Bacteria – These convert organic matter into something plants can use and sometimes have powerful relationships with the plants themselves.
- Fungi – You know fungi as mushrooms, but the important part of fungus is its system of rootlike threads running through the soil. These threads decompose matter just as bacteria does, but they also build soil nutrients in partnership with plants. Some might kill plants, but many others actually prevent diseases.
- Protozoa – These organisms eat bacteria, keeping the helpful bacteria in balance and releasing the nitrogen that plants need.

- Nematodes – Nematodes do some of the same things that protozoa do, and they also travel around spreading live bacteria and fungi through the soil. Some of them prevent diseases and provide food for helpful predators.
- Arthropods – These are insects that you can sometimes see, but often can't. Ants, beetles, sow bugs, spiders, mites, centipedes, and more all live together in the soil, chopping up materials and eating other bugs and fungus. They simultaneously mix the soil and make organic material more accessible to plants.
- Worms – Worms are the powerhouses. They eat the organic matter in the soil and their *castings* (droppings) are perfect plant food. Worms create thousands and thousands of pounds of casts per acre.

Organic Matter

All those living creatures feed off each other, but they need one thing to get started. Organic matter is at the bottom of their food chain, the fuel that keeps everything going. *Organic* in this sense means organisms: living and dead creatures and plants. When any kind of organic matter is added to the soil, all those living creatures get to work breaking it down, which adds nutrients to the soil that plants need. Once the matter breaks down completely, it becomes humus. Humus is organic matter that has decomposed so fully that whatever is left will not break down any further. Besides being the catalyst for all the biological processes that occur in the soil, organic matter is the stuff that holds water and prevents *runoff*. Runoff is exactly what it sounds like—rain or snow falls on the earth, but can't be absorbed and so it just runs off the surface. Without humus, the soil erodes and loses nutrients, leaving plants to die of thirst and starvation. Soil organisms are able to decompose organic matter at such a fast rate that continuing perpetually requires massive amounts of organic matter to maintain the same nutrient content and life cycle. In nature, the plants provide the input by dying and falling right back into the soil, but in farming this material is taken away and consumed by people. For example, according to the Natural Resources Conservation Service (NRCS), an acre of wheat must have at least two to three tons of organic matter or more added to it every year to maintain the same quality. That same wheat field has 30,000 miles (24,140 km) of roots just sucking up all those nutrients.

The Nitrogen Cycle

Life on Earth hangs in a careful balance. All organisms require nitrogen to live, and it is even part of our DNA. Most of the nitrogen available to us is found in the atmosphere, but it first has to be converted to a different chemical form for any organism to be able to use it. One of the single most important bacteria we know of today is *Rhizobium*, which lives in a symbiotic relationship with only some plants. It exists in nodules in the roots of legumes like beans and peas and *fixes* the nitrogen found in the soil so the plants in the vicinity can use it. Fixing it really means converting it into ammonium. Some other things can do this, too, such as blue-green algae, lightning, forest fires, and molten lava. Once the plants absorb the ammonium, they eventually die and decomposers move in. Most of the now-unusable nitrogen contained in the plant is converted back into ammonium again and released into the soil where other plants can use it, which is the optimum scenario. However, some of this ammonium doesn't make it to plants because other soil bacteria convert it into nitrates. Unlike ammonium, which binds to the soil, nitrates are loose and just wash out with water. This leads to a loss of soil fertility and creates a nitrate buildup in streams and groundwater. Some of this nitrate also turns into gas, which goes into the atmosphere to become smog and greenhouse gas. Once it does that, it will never be part of the nitrogen cycle again and is essentially lost.

Humans have more than doubled what would have been a relatively steady global nitrogen-fixing rate without our interference. By burning fossil fuels, growing mass quantities of legumes like soybeans, and through the use of synthetic fertilizer, we have pushed the nitrogen cycle beyond a sustainable level. Synthetic fertilizer was invented in the early 1900s and involves high temperatures and pressure to fix nitrogen, in much the same way that a cataclysmic natural event would. Chemical fertilizer makes up the vast majority of the fixed nitrogen we create, and while it can be used to grow more crops, it has disastrous consequences. While organic ammonium does leech nitrates into our drinking water, it is at a very low level that we barely notice. When chemical fertilizer leeches out, however, it creates extremely high and dangerous levels of nitrates in our drinking water. Nitrates lead to cancer and breathing problems for babies; they kill fish and change the biological balance of fragile coastal ecosystems. When emitted into the atmosphere, they become acid rain. The careful balance of the nitrogen cycle, which we depend on so completely for our survival, is in extreme danger. This may be the biggest argument against chemical-based farming.

Measuring Soil Health

Besides merely looking at the structure of the soil to see how much humus is there, we can measure the relative health of the soil by testing to see how acidic or alkaline it is. If you remember high school chemistry, soil testing uses the pH scale of 0 to 14, with low numbers being more acidic and high numbers being more alkaline. A pH of 7 is neutral, and most plants like 6 or 6.5. You can buy a soil testing kit from any garden supply store, and you will find that your soil will usually range from 5 (very acidic) to 8 (medium alkalinity).

Soils that are very acidic (with a lower pH) can't hold on to nitrogen well. The lower the pH, the more chemical nitrogen fertilizer will leech away. This affects natural nitrogen processes, as well—rhizobium just doesn't survive in highly acidic soil.

Plants need other minerals, as well, and a good soil testing kit will include tests for them. The solutions to these soil problems are not complex and don't require any kind of chemicals. If the soil is too acidic, you can add agricultural lime (a mineral) or wood ash, which is sprinkled on the soil at a rate of

20 pounds per 1,000 square feet, a little more if the soil has a more claylike consistency. Doing this also increases the potassium (K) levels, which we will talk about later. Other minerals (like sulfur) and trace elements (like manganese) tend to decrease as the soil becomes more acidic, and the most effective way to increase them is with compost, which coincidentally also decreases soil acidity. Compost and peat moss will raise the alkalinity and help with a host of other soil issues. As soil today becomes overused and overfertilized, it loses its ability to hold on to the nutrients that plants need. Compost is the solution to most of these issues.

The Right to Land

> "This we know. The earth does not belong to man; man belongs to the earth. This we know. All things are connected like the blood which unites one family. All things are connected."
>
> —Chief Seattle

Right-to-farm laws exist in most states and provinces in North America to protect farmers from nuisance lawsuits (not that they have been helpful lately, as we shall see), but the problem goes much deeper. Today the issue is not the right to farm, but the right to land access. In his "Land for People" speech in 1889, American economist Henry George said, "If you would realize what land is, think of what men would be without land. If there were no land, where would be the people? Land is not merely a place to graze cows or sheep upon, to raise corn or raise cabbage. It is the indispensable element necessary to the life of every human being. We are all land animals; our very bodies come from the land, and to the land they return again." Land is more than just an economic value. Humans need to have land to survive at a deep biological level.

According to a United Nations special report in 2010, Olivier De Schutter wrote, "Access to land and security of tenure are essential for the enjoyment of the right to food." In North America today, there are very few fighting for the legal right to land access, because culturally we see land ownership as a privilege. Is land a privilege or a right?

Not everyone is wasting time debating philosophical quandaries such as this. Groups like Reclaim the Fields, an organization of mostly young people in the UK who are determined to reclaim food production, have come together to take back land access. Sometimes this happens subversively, by planting seeds where they generally would not be noticed. Most of the time they are operating completely legal cooperative farms on community land to build successful gardens. Another UK organization, The Land Is Ours, is a campaign that has successfully seized many acres of land owned by government or corporations and converted it to agriculture. Their subsequent evictions and effective marketing have brought about land reform laws in many municipalities. In Africa the loss of land access has had much more dire consequences. Although more than 90 percent of land on that continent is free of any legal encumbrances, many women do not have land rights. This means that they lose their land if their husbands die, and yet according to Mary Kimani of the UN's *Africa Renewal*, they are responsible for 70 percent of Africa's farming. Women have banded together and negotiated for land access; without it they would live in extreme poverty, or worse.

In the United States, the federal government owns one-third of the land. In Canada, Queen Elizabeth II owns 90 percent of the land, and there is more unused land there than anywhere else in the world. North Americans are quick to fight for their access to recreational land for snowmobiling and hiking, but the movement to champion the right to agricultural land is almost nonexistent. The urban homesteading and urban farming movements are the closest thing America and Canada has to a real fight for land access.

Is land a right? If food and water are a human right, then so is land, because that's where those two absolutely necessary things come from. Landowners in the past have had a reputation as being oppressors, unfortunately, because land ownership brings status, and in some countries, royal titles. If everyone has access to land, then their status means nothing, and so these lords of the land are most often responsible for laws that take away everyone else's right to land. This could be readily seen in Britain from the Middle Ages onward with the adoption of feudalism. Conquering kings divided the land up between nobles and knights who rented it out to farmer peasants, but of course things there have been changing slowly for the better. Britain adopted a parliamentary democracy and the lords of the land began to lose some of their hold, although a third of the country is still in the hands of aristocrats. In the United States, however, land ownership has been getting more inequitable. In the 1860s, the Homestead Act made it possible for people to travel west, claim ownership of 160 acres of government land, and colonize the Pacific coast. This is exactly what the government wanted, for without citizens in place, America's hold on the western edge of the continent was not secure. Europeans were still colonizing the Americas, too, and many countries were trying to establish their piece of the pie. For the government, it was an economic decision; for Americans, it was about food and survival.

Eventually, 10 percent of all the territory in which American settlers staked claims was successfully transferred to private ownership through the Homestead Act. Approximately 400,000 people travelled the Oregon Trail battling unimaginable hardship until the completion of the transcontinental railroad in 1869. After that point, there was no disputing America's claim to the West, but the Act took land from hundreds of thousands of Native peoples who originally lived on it. Their struggle for land access is ongoing.

The Homestead Act was repealed in 1976, except in Alaska where it lasted until 1986. Westward expansion was no longer a priority, since Oregon and California had become states by that time. The back-to-the-land movement of the 1960s and 1970s saw people making claims once again through the Homestead Act. This sudden interest in free land made the US government decide to shut down the program, and land access has been a continuing battle ever since.

What to Do

Of course, the question is, what do we do about this situation? In the old days, people laid claim to property by squatting on it, that is, by occupying it for a period of time until it became theirs. But squatting now seems to have a negative connotation in North America, where squatter's rights are quite a bit different than they are in Europe, which sometimes favors the squatter over the property owner. Fortunately, access to land does not require land ownership, but simply the right to use land for sustainable agriculture without too much restriction. The single most inhibitive force to this is municipal bylaws, which in theory are designed to help the economy and protect citizens, but often hurt them because of their inability to change rapidly with current events. These city regulations may ensure safe building codes and proper use of public spaces, but they probably also prevent any kind of agricultural activity, even on a small scale.

The greatest microcosm of change in America today can be found amidst the desolation of Detroit, which was once a booming city at the center of car manufacturing with a population of 1.9 million. The population is now down to less than half that. The Detroit Works Project, created by the city government, but initiated by the citizens, is focused on sustainability and creating opportunity for green space. Citizens of Detroit who need access to land to grow food are slowly trying to tear down an invisible wall of bureaucracy keeping them from it. This means changing bylaws to allow urban farming, including the creation of an agricultural district just for commercial farming projects. Considering that the research and planning process took approximately two years and will take many more years to implement, it is imperative that other North American cities begin their own works projects now. It is much easier to implement change when your city is not in a state of desperation.

Peaches

By 2008, I had been writing about food for about six years. I was also twenty-seven, a married mother of two, and an immigrant to Canada. Motherhood was the major reason I had haplessly fallen into the task of writing about food (because I was suddenly paranoid about what I was feeding them), but it also hindered my chances of taking any action as an activist. It's quite a big step to go from wielding a pen to wielding a hoe. I struggled to find a matching pair of socks in the morning, let alone grow my own food or protest legislation.

My little family experienced a trifecta of crises that year involving marriage, finances, and goals that almost destroyed us. We were like any young couple that fights about money, except that we had married young and already had seven years under our belt. I was pregnant with our third child and we were renting an old house in a beautiful harbor city on Vancouver Island. You could see the ocean from the top floor bedroom window if you stood at just the right angle. My husband John had a reliable job, and the kids were happy at their little school. There was really no reason that we should have been in trouble except that we could never seem to get ahead, and our debt was becoming an unbearable burden.

The house was built in the 1920s, and we loved the hand-plastered curved ceilings even though the windows were drafty. In the spring, we built a hundred-square-foot raised garden. We discovered a walnut tree, blackberries, and salmon berries growing all around the yard. One day I was weeding the sunny backside of the house when I noticed a skinny sapling growing up against the stucco, much shorter than my five-foot height. As I looked closer, I realized this sad little tree was shockingly covered in hundreds of enormous fuzzy peaches. It almost frightened me that this three-foot-high stick had suspiciously exploded in glorious abundance. I picked one and hesitatingly took a bite, and my mouth exploded with the pure sweet nectar of the sun. I harvested fifty pounds of falling-off-the-tree peaches that day, and many fell to the ground to rot because we couldn't eat them fast enough. Store-bought fruit has absolutely nothing in common with the peach I ate that day, and I haven't bought one since. I believe that these peaches were a heritage variety grafted onto a much bigger tree decades ago, and when the tree was cut down the little grafted sapling somehow managed to survive. I imagined that they were a forgotten remnant of someone's World War II Victory Garden, a sixty-year-old treasure left for me to discover.

The garden became the inspiration and catalyst for the next step in solving our financial problems, and the resulting stress on our marriage. We built the garden and ate the food together and saved money. The crises began to look less bleak as we ate the most delicious tomatoes and peaches of our lives. And then with the money we saved, we began our adventure—in the Albatross.

Composting

"My whole life has been spent waiting for an epiphany, a manifestation of God's presence, the kind of transcendent, magical experience that lets you see your place in the big picture. And that is what I had with my first compost heap."

—Bette Midler

Compost is the greatest tool of any food activist. We may mourn the loss of farmland, feel disgust at the destruction of the soil, and shed tears over our diminished rights to land access, but one thing we can always do is make compost. It takes very little space, and even apartment dwellers can do it. Every person who is concerned about food should be composting.

The reason is simple. Compost is soil—and not just any soil. Compost is the ideal and optimum material for plants. It has all the microbes and bacteria and nutrients that are needed to produce life. It is absolutely necessary for success in growing vegetables. The apartment dweller might say, "But why make compost if I don't have space to grow food?" Soil is your contribution to food production wherever it might be. It can be used in the community garden, traded to your urban farmer who will be so grateful for it, or used for container gardens. Compost is the future currency of the local food movement.

The Composting Process

Composting can really be an art form, with the most skilled composter able to produce soil in just a few months. However, it doesn't have to be complicated. If you put plant material in your compost pile, it will begin to decay and in about six to eight months you will have usable compost no matter what you do. You just can't go wrong because bacteria, mold, and organisms are doing all the work.

There are three major compost methods:

Large Bin: Usually chosen by people who produce a lot of plant and vegetable waste from their big backyard garden. Three bins are built in a row and the new material is added only to the first bin. This pile is turned into the second bin after thirty days if the pile is at least three feet tall and three feet wide. After another thirty days, the material in the second bin is transferred to the third bin. By the time the pile has spent thirty days in the third bin, it should be done. This method takes two to three months to make usable compost.

Black Bin: Also known as the backyard composter, this is a black plastic bin that has two features: a lid on the top and a removable door on the bottom for removing compost. There are many different styles of composters, but as long as they are made of black plastic and have some ventilation holes and doors, they all work the same way. These bins are appropriate for kitchen scraps and smaller quantities of garden waste. The bin should sit on bare soil so that organisms from the ground can move into it; it should be near enough to the back door that you can easily add scraps from the kitchen; and it should be in direct sunlight, as the heat from the sun helps to break down the plant material. It should not be up against the house or fence, because spillage from frequent dumping of waste can damage nearby structures. Once full, the bin should be turned every couple of weeks for aeration. This method takes six to twelve months to make usable compost.

Worm Bin: Vermicomposting (or composting with worms) is useful to everyone, but particularly for apartment dwellers, because worm bins can be kept under the kitchen sink. It doesn't matter what the dimensions are, but 2' × 1.5' × 1' is usually a good size. You can buy a premade bin or make one out of a plastic bin by drilling drainage holes in the bottom and ventilation holes in the sides. The bin needs a lid and it's a good idea for it to sit on a deep tray or a larger bin to catch any drips, which are valuable as compost tea. You will have to purchase red wigglers or bait worms that don't mind living in tight spaces and eating a variety of foods. They prefer 70°F and need some moisture to get started, but with the lid on, they will stay fairly wet.

It's a good idea to add material to the bottom of any kind of compost pile or bin, which will keep an air space and help with aeration. Hedge trimmings, sticks, twigs, and other woody materials can work well for large bins and black bins. Worms prefer a bed that's a mixture of shredded newspaper and dry leaves.

After you have your bin set up, it's time to start adding material. Don't put any animal products into your compost, including meat, bones, dairy products, or eggs (except the shells). These will not decompose quickly and you may end up with maggots and mice. You also cannot add dog or cat feces. Worms are pickier, as you can see from the table. They don't like potatoes, citrus rinds, onion peels, acidic foods like tomatoes and pineapple, or bread. They just won't eat these scraps.

Things you can add to your compost:

Large and Black Bin	Worm Bin
Grass clippings	Shredded leaves
Weeds and plants	Shredded paper
Livestock manure	Coir (coconut husks)
Fruit and vegetable scraps	Fruit and vegetable scraps
Eggshells	Coffee grounds
Fall leaves	Tea bags
Straw	Egg shells
Chopped woody debris	
Newspaper or paper products	
Sawdust	
Shredded cardboard	
Seaweed	
Pet hair	
Soy milk	
Tea bags	
Crab and lobster shells	
Dryer lint	
Urine	

The Carbon/Nitrogen Ratio

Everything has a carbon/nitrogen ratio, or C:N ratio. The ideal compost pile has a 25–30:1 C:N ratio, and each material has its own ratio. Table scraps are normally 15:1 and manure is 20:1. It can be a bit complex to keep the pile at this perfect ratio. The easiest way to keep track of this is to categorize everything into Greens and Browns. Greens are the Nitrogen group and include fresh, green plants; fruit and vegetable scraps; seaweed; and fresh manure. Carbon is the Browns, including dry, dead material like paper, sawdust, and leaves. Simply add equal amounts of each to keep the right balance and allow the mixture to heat up. If you have the time, chopping everything into tiny pieces speeds up the decomposition process.

You will know when your compost is ready to harvest when it looks like soil. It should be dark and crumbly and have very few signs of food scraps. The material will have shrunk down quite a bit and won't smell bad anymore. You can add this material straight to your garden by stirring it into the first inch of soil or just sprinkling it on top. The Worm Bin requires a little more effort. After three to five months, you won't see much bedding left. There are several methods that people use, but the best way is to dump the whole thing out. You have to do this from time to time anyway, so you might as well do it when you harvest the castings. You need a tarp and a sunny day or a big light. Just dump the bin upside down on the tarp and wait for the worms to escape from the light towards the bottom of the pile. Remove the castings from the top of the pile and stir it around gently to remove anything else. You will be left with a bunch of worms and a small amount of castings. Put new bedding in the bin, return the worms to their home, and give them a big meal.

CHAPTER TWO

Controlling Genetics

"We've got ninety-nine percent the same genes as any other person. We've got ninety percent the same as a chimpanzee. We've got thirty percent the same as a lettuce. Does that cheer you up at all? I love that about the lettuce. It makes me feel I belong."

—Caryl Churchill, A Number

A Thousand Years in a Seed

"It always amazes me to look at the little, wrinkled brown seeds and think of the rainbows in 'em," said Captain Jim. "When I ponder on them seeds I don't find it nowise hard to believe that we've got souls that'll live in other worlds. You couldn't hardly believe there was life in them tiny things, some no bigger than grains of dust, let alone colour and scent, if you hadn't seen the miracle, could you?"

—L. M. Montgomery, *Anne's House of Dreams*

All food comes from seeds. Without seeds, and the plants they become, animals would be unable to produce milk, eggs, and meat. Humans have a wildly variable diet, and now with the miracle of transportation, we can eat any plant species from anywhere in the world. We have voracious appetites, insisting on bananas for breakfast all year round in the middle of North Dakota, and juicy green lettuce in the middle of the desert. We demand apples, fresh and crisp, everywhere and anytime.

The apple is an amazing fruit. It is healthful and packaged perfectly for eating. People have grown apples for more than eight thousand years. How many varieties of apples have you eaten? You have probably only had a few: Red and Golden Delicious, Spartan, Gala, Granny Smith, and Fuji. This is because only one hundred types of apples are grown commercially in North America, and only fifteen varieties make up 90 percent of that. Considering the fact that there are at least 7,500 types of apples in the world, ranging from the size of a grape to several pounds, and covering all imaginable flavors, most of us have barely touched the tip of the iceberg in the apple world.

At the very beginning of recorded history, humans started to develop the many different varieties we enjoy today, but what is unique about apples is that the seed will not grow the same apple that it came from. Each apple is the result of crossing two different kinds of apples to produce a child like its parent. If the apple self-pollinates, it creates an apple unlike itself, and so breeds had to be cross-pollinated and experimented with. This is how successful varieties were discovered and saved. In this way, the apple became not only a staple food for all humans; it became enmeshed in our culture and mythology. The apples we eat today are the result of thousands of years of effort by possibly millions of people over generations of time. Each variety has its own special qualities—its hardiness to certain types of weather, pest, or disease; its size, flavor, or texture; whether it should be eaten raw or cooked.

Seeds of *cultivated varieties*, or plants that have been grown and bred by humans, are genetically diverse. Genetic diversity is held in the DNA of a species. There are millions of species of edible vegetables and fruits, and each one holds DNA that contains millions of characteristics that can adapt to any situation. For example, in your DNA is a complex set of options that determine everything from the color of your skin to your special affinity for the violin, and each person simply displays whatever characteristic your family line dictates. Plants are no different. The more genetic diversity a species has, the more likely it will be able to adapt to an uncertain future.

In this time of relative security and health, it may seem inconsequential to worry about the survival of a single variety of carrot. What could nature possibly throw our way that would make a certain species of tomato essential? What global disaster could be so critical that a specific variety of potato becomes important?

In the fall of 1845 just such an event occurred, and it was so disastrous that it has become part of our cultural history, even though most people today have no idea what happened. At that time, Ireland had a population of about 8 million people, most of them living in extreme poverty, with an average life expectancy of forty years. Many of these people fed themselves by farming. The agrarian life was not as pleasant as it is in North America today, but most of its problems were the same, including the struggle to access land. Most of these farmers were tenants who borrowed the use of land from wealthy lords and could be kicked off the land at any time. Because of this, farmers produced crops that had a very low monetary value. The potato became the perfect crop for Ireland. Each acre produced about twelve tons per year, and this, along with a little buttermilk from the cow and some cabbage, could provide enough nutrition for the farmer and his family. By 1845, more than 3 million farmers lived off potatoes alone, and this monoculture system seemed to be prospering.

But it didn't last. A spore, borne on the wind from ships that had travelled to North America, infested the potatoes with a blight that turned the leaves black. When the desperate farmers dug the potatoes up, they were relieved to see what looked like perfectly healthy potatoes beneath the dead plants. Within a few days, however, their hopes were dashed. When exposed to air, the potatoes turned black and rotted. Millions of people faced total crop failure within a few months, and starvation was imminent without a root cellar full of potatoes for the winter.

To alleviate the problem, England's prime minister worked to repeal the Corn Laws, which were a set of laws that had placed high tariffs on grains. Cheap grain was available to be brought to Ireland if only the Corn Laws hadn't fixed the price at an exorbitant rate. However, the English business world fought against the repeal and the Corn Laws stayed in place. Ireland did produce major grain crops during this time, but these were controlled by the equivalent of an English marketing board. The grain was shipped to England and wholesalers pocketed the money. Prime Minister Peel was so hated for his attempt to help the Irish by hurting English trade that he was forced to resign, and subsequent retaliatory legislation removed all government aid from Ireland. People believed that the crop failures were temporary, but they weren't. The crops failed the next year, and the next. Within six years, more than a million families (about 12 percent of the population) starved to death, slowly and painfully.

Potato blight still exists and still threatens potato crops. Today, potatoes are treated with fungicides as many as fifteen times throughout the growing season. There are now potatoes, such as the Sarpo, that have been bred to resist the fungus. Developed by the Sávári family in Hungary over several generations, not only is the Sarpo blight resistant, it is more resilient in general than other potatoes. The potato blight fungus has continued to morph and change and become resistant to fungicides over the years, but people have continued to develop the Sarpo to ensure that it remains resistant to all forms of blight. This is one of the best examples of practical grassroots plant breeding, as an alternative to genetic modification, to solve a common agricultural problem.

Nature is never stable or predictable. The environment we live in changes in the blink of an eye, and microscopic creatures are simultaneously the means of our survival and the bane of our existence. If history has taught us anything, it has proven that monoculture will fail over and over again, and that the government can really do nothing to protect farmers, no matter how many programs and marketing boards it creates. Even more importantly, a single potato variety can mean the difference between life and death.

The Real Problems With Genetic Modification

"As far as genetic engineering for food, that is the great experiment that has failed. [GM companies] literally have the entire world market against them. All those dreams . . . the blind will see, the lame will walk . . . has turned out to be science fiction. They are basically chemical companies selling more chemicals. They've been able to spread these herbicide-promoting plants around because it is more convenient for farmers who can just mass-spray their crops. But they've given absolutely nothing to the consumer while causing more chemical pollution and contamination." —Andrew Kimbrell, executive director of the Center for Food Safety (USA)

Genetically modified (or GM) plants came into existence in a different way from the seeds you buy at the garden center. Unlike the thousands of species of plants that humans have cultivated throughout thousands of years, those that are genetically modified come out of a lab in a few years. There are about five companies in the world that dominate this industry: Bayer, Dow, DuPont, Monsanto, and Syngenta. These labs experiment on plants by inserting genetic material or DNA directly into a species' DNA to give those plants traits that make them grow bigger, pest-resistant, or impervious to herbicides. At first glance, this sounds simple enough, but genetic modification rarely uses genes from the same species. Potatoes, for example, might be introduced with DNA from a bean, bacteria, or even a pig.

There are many people who believe that on some level this genetically engineered food must be harmful to eat. The idea of some kind of "monster pig-corn" frightens people, as maybe it should, but as of today, there is very little evidence supporting the idea that eating GM food has harmful side effects. There have not been enough comprehensive, legitimate studies by unbiased sources to prove that GM foods are either harmful or safe for human consumption. But the fact that not enough concrete study exists is troubling in itself. When the FDA approves a new medication, the drug company that makes it must prove not only the drug's effectiveness, but also maintain a list of its side effects. Doctors use this list to weigh the risks versus the benefits. All drugs have side effects, but often their risks are minimal compared to the disease they treat. Unfortunately, no such process exists for GM food.

But even if we can't prove the direct health risks of GM foods, we can still look at how they have affected soil, farmers, and the food supply in general. Here are the facts, according to the USDA:

1. As of 2011, 94 percent of soybean, 81 percent of cotton, and about 80 percent of corn crops were genetically modified.

2. This overwhelming takeover of soybeans, cotton, and corn happened within a very short, fifteen-year span. Genetic modification only began in 1996.

3. This represents a huge amount of farmland. There are more than 72 million acres planted with corn in the United States, which means that 68 million acres are growing GM corn. This is roughly the size of the state of Colorado.

4. There are two kinds of GM corn, Bt corn and regular GM corn, which are chosen by farmers either to kill pests or reduce weeds.

    a. Bt corn contains bacteria called *Bacillus thuringiensis*. This releases spores that kill insects when they eat the corn.

    b. Weed-resistant corn is sold under the name Round-Up Ready. This corn is able to survive strong dosages of lethal herbicide so that all plant life around it dies.

Besides producing the majority of the seed for 90 percent of the US corn market, Round-Up is also made by Monsanto, which is no surprise, since the company has such a big stake in the bioengineering industry. Monsanto's game is two-pronged. The Round-Up Ready corn is not intrinsically resistant to weeds. It requires a heavy dose of herbicide to thrive. Currently, GM corn can only do one of two things: resist pests by killing them or survive the Round-Up that kills the weeds around it. Since these are the two major risks of growing corn, farmers jump on this as a solution to all their problems. But is it really a solution or just another problem in the making?

If we look back more than forty years ago, we'll remember that Monsanto was creating DDT and Agent Orange for the Vietnam War. Soldiers had to machete their way through dense jungle, which was exhausting and left them vulnerable to attack. Agent Orange became the means of removing this jungle. Named for the orange barrels it came in, Agent Orange contained dioxin, one of the most toxic chemicals threatening humans. Dioxin stays in fatty tissue a very long time, harming various organs and systems of the body, and because of this it is very difficult to control or do anything about. Even at low levels, it damages the immune system and vital organs and causes miscarriage and sterility, birth defects, and especially cancer. In fact, according to the World Health Organization, it is the most potent cancer-causing chemical known today.

Dioxin naturally occurs as a result of erupting volcanoes or forest fires, but most dioxin found in the world occurs from industrial processing. Paper mills using bleach to whiten paper and waste incinerators burning trash create dioxin as a by-product that is released into the environment. Once free, it travels all over the world depositing itself in soil and on everything. All dairy products, meat, and fish contain dioxins, which are monitored by the FDA to ensure the levels don't get too high for human consumption. When Agent Orange was released over Vietnam from airplanes, much of it was carried to other parts of the world by wind or water. Six years and 21 million gallons of Agent Orange later, the Vietnamese people suffer a high cancer rate and related health problems, including terrible genetic defects. US soldiers didn't fare much better. In the 1980s, Vietnam War veterans sued manufacturers for damages due to Agent Orange, and in 1984 they received some remuneration: $180 million was settled out of court, with almost half paid by Monsanto alone. These soldiers won this settlement because it was proven that Monsanto, and other manufacturers, had falsified research data to make Agent Orange seem safe when people were exposed to it, but veterans were dismayed at the way the case was handled. Each veteran was to receive $12,000 paid out over ten years (Chambers). Almost 90,000 veterans filed disability claims with the Department of Veterans Affairs for serious respiratory disorders, cancer, and unusually high rates of miscarriage and birth defects. Up until 1993, only 486 victims had been awarded health care and benefits for Agent Orange exposure (Fleischer), and until 2010 there was no way they could get compensation for the terrible diseases they were facing. It took forty-eight years for the government to recognize the damage these soldiers had endured and take care of them. Monsanto and other companies, however, have never admitted to the connection between Agent Orange and the soldiers' illnesses. Jill Montgomery, a spokesperson for Monsanto in 2004 said, "We are sympathetic with people who believe they have been injured and understand their concern to find the cause, but reliable scientific evidence indicates that Agent Orange is not the cause of serious long-term health effects." (Fawthrop) This does not bode well for the millions of Vietnamese people who have still not been compensated at all.

After the end of the war, Monsanto struggled to recover as a company. With their biggest product now obsolete, they had to reinvent themselves. During the time that Agent Orange was being developed, they had also created glyphosate, another herbicide that is slightly gentler and has a much shorter half-life. They marketed this as Round-Up.

Most farmers now generally use herbicides and have done so since their creation during World War II. However, weeds often develop a resistance to herbicides over time and come back stronger. Farmers who use herbicides still have to till in the weeds, or turn them under the soil. However, as we unfortunately learned during the Dust Bowl, too much tilling causes dramatic soil erosion. When you have a hundred acres of corn it's not possible to pull the weeds by hand, so you can spray them with chemicals, but you have to be very careful or you could kill your entire crop. Monsanto began advertising Round-Up Ready corn as an ecological product that would save the soil, because farmers would no longer have to till the weeds in, the chemicals wouldn't damage the corn, and the weeds would just shrivel up and die. Theoretically this would be more profitable for the farmer, who could apply less herbicide, work fewer hours, and reap a greater yield.

Why anyone would trust a company that started its career by falsifying scientific research that resulted in the long-term destruction of the health of millions of Vietnamese people and American soldiers is questionable. But the fact remains that Monsanto has become the chief supplier to the American grain industry, the chief driver behind lobbying for FDA approval of GM products, and the chief motivator behind most GM research. But is GM really better for the farmer, as Monsanto claims?

In 2009 the Union of Concerned Scientists published a comprehensive report on GM crops titled "Failure to Yield." As you may guess, it is not in favor of genetically engineered crops. The UCS is not some small group of fanatical quacks. Started by professors and science students at MIT, the Union of Concerned Scientists is a collaboration of 250,000 scientists and citizens who have made it their business to fact-check technology. They make sure that companies have scientific integrity, especially in terms of the environment.

"Failure to Yield" analyzed twenty years of scientific research and thirteen years of commercial production reports and concluded that genetically engineered plants don't yield more and aren't more profitable than any other kind of crop. While GM corn and soybean yields have increased, they found that this has more to do with better technology in the growing process and corn breeding than anything having to do with biotechnology. Even Bt corn, which is supposed to prevent destruction by killing the corn borer caterpillar, only yields about 7 to 12 percent more corn if the infestation is very high. If the corn borers are just moderately infesting the crop, there is no advantage at all. This failure to fulfill promises is specious because GM seeds are marketed as the only solution to the world's growing food crises. Bill Gates, the most prominent and public promoter of genetically modified foods, has invested in 500,000 shares of Monsanto and spent billions on genetic engineering. He spoke at the UN International Fund for Agriculture and Development in February 2012 in support of genetically engineered seeds, saying, "We have to think hard about how to start taking advantage of the digital revolution that is driving innovation including in farming. If you care about the poorest, you care about agriculture. We believe that it's possible for small farmers to double and in some cases even triple their yields in the next twenty years while preserving the land."

From a business standpoint, it is doubtful that GM crops would be a solution to poverty. GM seed costs four times as much as regular seed, and you can't legally save the seed because it is patented. Poor farmers help alleviate costs by saving seed, and when they can't, they have to come up with money every spring. They often get in debt to finance the spring planting, and then they must factor in the cost of Round-Up at least a few times a year to kill the weeds. Finally, GM supporters must prove that yields are actually higher, while twenty years of research has proven that they aren't. Is this a solution to poverty and the food crises or to Monsanto's shrinking bank account?

The real trouble with GM crops, however, is that they cause *genetic drift*. Hawaii, with its beautiful warm climate and relatively flat and fertile ground, has become a haven for bioengineering testing. Thousands of acres of open-air fields are devoted to testing new types of corn, bananas, and even papayas. However, the regular crops on the island are becoming contaminated with GM strains. This is a simple natural phenomenon:

The genetically engineered crops may be high tech and kill pests and resist chemicals, but they still behave like regular plants. They produce pollen, which is carried off by bees or the wind and fertilizes plants elsewhere. This normal process has been completely ignored by scientists working on GM development. Perhaps we can excuse the drift of corn or soybeans approved by the government, but when testing new strains, should the plants be grown in the open air where they can spread everywhere? It's the same as running a science experiment in the street and allowing it to spill all over the neighborhood, without caring about the consequences. It's just bad science.

This has acutely affected the organic papaya industry in Hawaii. Organic papayas grown from non-GM organic seed have become genetically modified because of cross-pollination. Japan now requires that all organic Hawaiian papayas be tested before import, and South Korea has stopped importing them altogether. Some farmers have spent thousands of dollars for organic certification, only to lose it overnight after a single lab test. The attitude from the bioengineering community has been that the new papayas are better, so why grow the old ones anyway? The genetic drift into organic crops was discovered in 2004, and to date the organic papaya farmers have not been able to protect their varieties or get compensation. In the end, many organic papaya farms have simply had to shut down.

This drift doesn't just impact organic farmers. It changes the entire ecosystem. The testing of backyard and farm papaya trees by the University of Hawaii in 2006 showed that in some places at least 50 percent of all the papayas are now GM. Even more alarming was the discovery that the university's own papaya seed bank had been contaminated. The same story has been repeated over and over again in corn, canola, and soybean production. Even nonorganic farmers that don't have to worry about cross-pollination have been surprised and angry that they aren't growing the plants they intended to. The right to grow any kind of seed you want has been taken away, and it is completely out of anyone's control. Is this really about saving the world from starvation, or is it about profits and controlling the supply of seeds? This so-called science masquerading as a humanitarian effort is working toward the destruction of a free and healthy food supply.

Chemicals and Cancer

"One must not forget that recovery is brought about not by the physician, but by the sick man himself. He heals himself, by his own power, exactly as he walks by means of his own power, or eats, or thinks, breathes or sleeps."

—Georg Groddeck, *The Book of the It*, 1923

It seems appropriate, in the midst of all of this talk about GM and chemicals, to talk about cancer. Chances are that you know someone who has had cancer. It is the second leading cause of death in the United States (after heart disease) and the leading cause of death in Canada. One in eight women will be diagnosed with breast cancer, and one in eighteen people will develop colon cancer, so the odds are that you or someone close to you will have it at some point. While cancer rates are mostly rising because of our aging population, even young people are affected more than they used to be. This growing cancer plague can no longer be explained away as an age thing or even just a genetic thing. There is growing evidence that it is related to our food.

Eating processed meats like bacon, sausage, and sandwich meat has been proven to increase your chances of pancreatic cancer by 17 percent if you eat them regularly (Gallagher). Add red meat like hamburger and your risk of colon cancer jumps to 36 percent (National Cancer Institute). Most North Americans eat red and processed meat almost every day, so the simple solution is to eat less meat.

CONTROLLING GENETICS

With vegetables and fruit, however, things get a little trickier. As of today, no concrete link has been found between eating manufactured pesticides and a higher risk of cancer. Most people aren't aware that fruit and vegetables also make their own natural pesticides, and some of these are toxic. For example, basil contains estragole and benzyl acetate, and apples contain caffeic acid, all possible carcinogens to humans (that is, possibly cancer-causing). In fact, according to a study at the University of California, Berkeley, researchers found that out of the total chemicals in our diets, 99.99 percent are natural, and about half of them are possible carcinogens. On top of this, cooking food also creates toxic chemicals. According to a meta-analysis at the same university, there are more than a thousand chemicals in coffee, many of which are produced just by the act of roasting it (Gold). Of the thirty chemicals that have been tested for carcinogenic properties, twenty-one have come back positive. This means that despite the best organic growing practices, your fair trade organic coffee still has cancer-causing chemicals in it due to how it's made.

Humans have natural defenses against these kinds of chemicals, and our immune systems are designed to cope with many of them. However, we are not really designed to eat foods that have been genetically tampered with, and some argue that we aren't evolved enough to eat some of the foods that have been introduced more recently. Our immune system is still based on a hunter-gatherer diet, and when we mess with that, our risk for cancer goes up. If you avoid fruits and vegetables because you can't afford organic food, you are actually increasing your risk of getting cancer. Eating fresh fruit and vegetables prevents cancer, whether they have chemicals or not. But some plants that we eat today were not part of the hunter-gatherer diet, and are also not part of many people's bioregional ancestry. For example, tomatoes, potatoes, coffee, tea, kiwi fruit, avocados, and mangoes did not become part of our diet until the last couple of thousand years, but our immune systems haven't caught up to the toxic chemicals in these fruits and vegetables. There are ten thousand natural pesticides found in the common North American diet, but only seventy or so have been tested thoroughly for toxicity. Apples, lettuce, pears, coffee, beer, cinnamon, carrots, black pepper, and nutmeg all contain levels of natural chemicals that are riskier to your health than any synthetic chemical residue they may have. When compared to the synthetic pesticides used on food today, almost all the natural pesticides rank higher in toxicity. Potatoes, a major staple in most people's diets, were only introduced to the rest of the world a few hundred years ago, and they contain the natural pesticides solanine and chaconine. Both of these are found in the blood of people who eat potatoes, and these chemicals are the source of serious reproductive problems at high doses. Solanine is the reason we have to cook potatoes, and why we can't eat green ones. A very bitter taste and green flesh are good indicators that the solanine levels are very high. Even though it is known that solanine causes health problems, no study has been done on the long-term effects of low levels of the chemical. The reasoning is that people have been eating them for so long with relative safety, so there's no reason to find out if solanine causes problems.

What does all this have to do with cancer? It means that as of today, there is no way to know whether the cancer you get is the result of natural chemicals or synthetic ones, and it is highly likely that the natural ones are just as guilty. This doesn't mean that synthetic pesticides are good, however. As companies like Monsanto develop stronger chemicals and dump more and more on our crops, it's obvious that they are going to have an adverse effect on us. There is also a very real and possibly much more important danger. Because these GM crops are created to contain their own pesticides (such as the corn-borer-killing corn), how do we know that our bodies can resist that chemical? The argument that we can use fewer pesticides by giving the corn a natural pesticide is absurd. They are both the same thing and have the exact same risk, and bioengineers are just trading one pesticide for another. The companies and scientists who develop them know this. It's the clearest proof that the company is not interested in ecology or feeding a growing population, but rather in patenting and owning the food supply and covering it up with clever marketing.

Studies of skeletons and mummies have consistently shown that in ancient times, cancer was quite rare, mostly due to the fact that the average age of death was thirty-six years old. There is a growing movement to eat a "Paleolithic diet." The rules are simple: eat foods that you could only eat raw (to avoid natural toxins), eat organic and wild foods, and eat a high percentage of wild and pasture-fed meat. Followers of this diet avoid grain, dairy, legumes, salt, sugar, and processed oils. In many ways, this plan is similar to any low-carbohydrate, high-protein diet like the one Robert Atkins promoted. However, there is little evidence that a) Paleolithic people were healthier because of their diet and b) Paleolithic people ate these foods in the first place. Evidence shows that ancient people ate a wildly varying diet based on wherever they happened to be at the time. As various groups settled down and established civilization, they tended to eat what grew best in their climate. Mediterranean people were eating wheat and greens, while Vikings were eating more meat and barley. Asians were eating fish and rice, and Africans were eating tubers and birds. These are generalizations, but the human diet has never followed one pattern. There is a growing field of nutritional science that is trying to determine if different gene pools have different immunities to different diets. There is a strong possibility that if your ancestors didn't eat avocados, you probably shouldn't eat avocados, but if they did, you should.

One fact remains. Until a hundred years ago, we did not add chemicals to our food, which was already full of natural chemical defenses. Until fifty years ago, we pulled it fresh out of the ground from not very far away. Until twenty years ago, we didn't genetically modify our food. We may be living longer, but we are now battling cancer at unprecedented levels, and it has become an ever-present part of our lives. Prevention is our only defense, which means limiting our exposure to chemicals, eating way less red and processed meats, and much more fruit and vegetables. And perhaps we should consider the idea that an extremely varied diet from all over the globe is not healthier, but actually injurious, when genetically we are built to thrive on a few local foods like our ancestors.

A Family Project

I had my third daughter in the summer of 2009, and I think my peach diet might have influenced her sunny disposition. That year, we also made a decision to find a way to get some land and grow food. My little garden just wasn't enough to keep me satisfied. We had no money, we were in debt, and we didn't own anything of value. But we knew we had to completely change everything about our lives, we had to somehow get out of debt, and we had to work together on a project if we were going to save our marriage. So, we did what anyone would do. We bought a bus to live in.

Cheap school buses are in short supply in Canada, so we found one on eBay located in Nevada. The price was $4,000, which at that time was an enormous amount of money for us. John flew down to Lake Tahoe and drove it home, white knuckled and sick with nervousness, all the way back to Vancouver Island.

We pulled out the seats and the flooring to the metal shell, sanded off the rust, sealed it, and laid down insulation and plywood on the floor. We bought a small space heater and began our ultimate camping adventure.

John continued working at his regular job and then came back and worked on the bus in the evening while the rest of us cooked outside and played at washing our laundry by hand. We parked it at the homes of various friends and family who had a little bit of space for a large Blue Bird. Then fall rolled around and we weren't done building yet. It began to get cold, and we were mostly done, but the bus still needed a furnace and other things. We rented a basement suite and wondered if we had made a terrible mistake. Our bus was

ridiculously nice—it was becoming an amazing thing—and yet it was a much bigger project than we could have possibly imagined. We also hadn't really been able to figure out why we had a bus in the first place. We considered the idea of buying land, but real estate prices in British Columbia were just so high, and we weren't sure that we wanted to be those people who live in the boonies in a bus.

The next spring we rallied ourselves and began again. Living in the bus was so cheap, we needed only $12,000 a year to support our family of five. With John working, we were able to pour enough into the bus to finish it off. We now had a very comfortable motor home that had cost about $35,000 to renovate, but that was cheap for something we owned outright. Most importantly, we had gotten out of debt by living so frugally.

We had accomplished two of our goals: We had saved our marriage by doing something impossible together, and we had scrambled out of our financial hole. We went from being in debt to owning an asset worth something. It took two years, but we felt that finally we would be able to do the things we wanted to do, whatever they might be. The biggest stumbling block for anyone trying to gain access to land is money, and now without debt and with very low living costs, we would be able to take all our extra income and pour it into something meaningful. We also had a traveling home that could be put down anywhere we wanted. We felt free.

Genetic Use Restriction Technology

"If you control the oil, you control the country; if you control food, you control the population."

—Henry Kissinger

If pesticide use, genetic drift, and mediocre yields of GM crops aren't big enough problems by themselves, the solutions that scientists have come up with to solve these problems only create more issues. Monsanto maintains a database of farmers using their seeds and conducts random tests of other farms nearby. If a neighboring field is found to contain GM varieties caused simply by genetic drift, the company feels that it has every right to go after the farmer for payment since it owns the patent on what is being grown. Biotechnology researchers funded by GM corporations have proposed *genetic use restriction technology* or GURTs.

Scientists have developed the technology to make plants self-destruct. A GURT is simply a genetic modification that makes a crop unable to reproduce. This strategy is problematic because most GM crops are grains, and the product we eat is the actual seed of the wheat and corn. If you take away the wheat's ability to reproduce, you also take away its ability to generate a kernel of wheat. This problem has inspired the idea of creating crops that regenerate by growing *tillers* (or self-propagating shoots) that pop out of the ground instead of using pollen. But this, in turn, has created a whole new set of issues to combat. If you take away the pollen and make the crops self-propagating, you are affecting a vast network of organisms that rely on that ecosystem. Wheat fields have replaced prairie and grassland in North America, but they essentially function the same way for organisms that live there. Changing the fundamental processes of reproduction was considered too difficult, as the repercussions could not be determined.

So instead, terminator seeds have been proposed by a major cotton seed breeder. This is a way of forcing plants to produce sterile seeds. This type of seed has been marketed as a solution to stopping the spread of GM genes everywhere. As Monsanto says on its own website, "GURTs can be used to limit the use or spread of specific genetic material in agriculture. For example, technology developers can invest in beneficial traits and utilize GURT to ensure specific traits are available only to farmers wanting to pay for and use the traits. GURTs also help with the stewardship of biotech crops by offering a means to ensure that biotech genetic material is present only in intended agricultural settings." At first glance, this plan may seem harmless enough. After all, how could these seeds hurt the environment if they don't reproduce?

Of course, it's not as simple as it sounds. The technology doesn't work automatically, and the plants have three genes that do three different jobs. The first is a toxin that kills only the seed after it develops, the second is a DNA sequence that prevents the toxin from killing the seed until a trigger agent activates it, and the third is an enzyme that automatically kills the offspring of a plant at the right time, after it is planted and activated. The activating trigger agent is tetracycline, the commonly used antibiotic. Monsanto can continue creating more seed by growing generations and generations of cotton, but as soon as they want to sell the seed, they simply soak it in antibiotics and the farmer won't be able to save any of it for future crops.

Unfortunately, terminator seeds aren't 100 percent foolproof. No matter what scientists do, genetic drift still happens, less often, of course, but DNA still persists in traveling. Scientists are not just battling a little unruly plant behavior; they are waging a war against thousands of years of evolution that guarantees the continuation of a species no matter what nature can throw at it. To scientists, this genetic drift would not be a problem at all because, after a single generation, the contaminated crops would die off and farmers could start again fresh. There would be no continuation of the GM contamination. To environmentalists and advocates, however, this poses a huge problem to farmers and the surrounding ecosystems, as the following story will illustrate.

The patent for GURTs, which was granted in March 1998, is held by Delta and Pine Land and the US Department of Agriculture. It was in development long before GM seeds had ever been marketed, because the scientists behind GM research knew that genetic drift would be a problem. By May 1998, Monsanto was trying to purchase Delta and Pine Land while Delta and Pine continued to take out more joint patents with the USDA. The original agreement between Delta and Pine Land and the USDA stated that the former had exclusive licensing rights, and the USDA would earn 5 percent of the sales on any commercial product sold using the GURT technology. Meanwhile the USDA had to defend its position because the agency's stake in the matter created worldwide controversy. USDA spokesperson Willard Phelps told Rural Advancement Foundation International (an advocate for family farms) that the goal of terminator technology was "to increase the value of proprietary seed owned by US seed companies and to open up new markets in Second and Third World countries." This statement created even more controversy, and in 1999 Monsanto felt it necessary to make a public statement that it would not commercialize the terminator technology, saying, "Though we do not yet own any sterile seed technology, we think it is important to respond to those concerns at this time by making clear our commitment not to commercialize gene protection systems that render seed sterile" (Shapiro). Monsanto successfully took over Delta and Pine Land and its subsidiaries in thirteen countries in 2006 and became the proud owner of Delta and Pine Land's share of the GURT patent.

The attitudes held by Monsanto's scientists and spokespeople illustrate that the company does not put that much stock in genetic drift or the environment. While the company would like the right to make its seeds sterile, it doesn't care if its seeds spread GM material everywhere. It is easy to imagine the results of the legalization of terminator seeds. Grain farmers all around the world save seed for future seasons. Not having to purchase seed every spring is often the only thing keeping them in business. Pushing this technology on the Third World is obviously unethical, but add to that the risk of genetic drift sterilizing a neighboring crop and it becomes criminal. This is a massive infringement on the rights of farmers and a threat to the free and secure continuation of the food supply. No less than a billion people in the world save grain seed, and that right would be taken away from them if the GURT technology were approved for commercial use.

There are other risks to think about as well. In March 2008, the United Nations met to formulate a recommendation on GURTs based on years of analysis of scientific data, and had this to say:

> . . . in the current absence of reliable data on genetic use restriction technologies, without which there is an inadequate basis on which to assess their potential risks, and in accordance with the precautionary approach, products incorporating such technologies should not be approved by Parties for field testing until appropriate scientific data can justify such testing, and for commercial use until appropriate, authorized and strictly controlled scientific assessments with regard to, inter alia, their ecological and socio-economic impacts and any adverse effects for biological diversity, food security and human health have been carried out in a transparent manner and the conditions for their safe and beneficial use validated.

This stance was based on not only the potential economic damage to Third World farmers, but also the process itself. The toxin within the plants is possibly toxic to humans, and if not humans, could surely be toxic to myriad other creatures. It could also cause allergic reactions and the food could be nutritionally different, which could potentially prevent us from absorbing vital nutrients. Not to mention, the incredibly large quantities of antibiotics could create resistant viruses and bacteria. The trouble is, as the UN report pointed out, we just don't know all the possible adverse effects of the commercialization of terminator technology.

What is most dangerous about this scenario is that it has become a political issue, almost entirely out of the hands of citizens. Monsanto has only to lobby the government to gain FDA approval, something the company has been successful doing partly because it's already in bed with the USDA. While Monsanto was publicly pledging to never commercialize terminator seeds, it was pouring money into research and development of its so-called Technology Protection System. Vice President of Technology Transfer Harry Collins at Delta and Pine Land (now called Deltapine) wrote in a legal letter to industry shareholders in 2000: "We've continued right on with work on the Technology Protection System. We never really slowed down. We're on target, moving ahead to commercialize it. We never really backed off." So, who's working for whom? The corporation working for the government, or vice versa?

The USDA Works for Corporations?

"The USDA is not our ally here. We have to take matters into our own hands, not only by advocating for a better diet for everyone—and that's the hard part—but by improving our own. And that happens to be quite easy. Less meat, less junk, more plants."

—Mark Bittman, author, E.G. Conference 2007,
What's Wrong with What We Eat

I don't think that anyone reading this book has missed the fact that the USDA is working for the good of corporations rather than consumers and small farmers. In the matters of bioengineered foods and organic regulation, the USDA has clearly sided with business to the detriment of safety, real science, or even what farmers want. Ron Hoggan, author of *Dangerous Grains*, wrote, "Because the USDA's function is largely the promotion of agriculture and agricultural products, there is a clear conflict of interest inherent in any USDA claim of healthful benefits arising from any agricultural product. Popular beliefs and politically motivated promotion, not science, continue to dictate dietary recommendations, leading to debilitating and deadly diseases that are wholly or partly preventable."

I would argue that the USDA isn't interested in promoting agriculture, but rather the middlemen, the companies who process and sell agricultural products. It's not really a secret that the people working in government seem exceptionally connected to the corporations they are protecting. Let's take a look at who's who at the USDA:

Tom Vilsack, Secretary of Agriculture. The current head of the USDA has a long history of supporting every corporate interest that is the opposite of sustainable and healthy, stretching back to his time as governor of Iowa. This includes GMOs, Monsanto, and processors who specialize in abuses of the system. The Biotechnology Industry Organization named him Governor of the Year in 2001.

Dr. Robert T. Frayley, USDA technical advisor. Frayley was also simultaneously executive vice president and chief technology officer at Monsanto. According to *Forbes*, his compensation from Monsanto in 2010 was $4.7 million.

Catherine Woteki, Under Secretary for Research, Education, and Economics. She previously worked as the global director of scientific affairs at Mars, Inc., managing the company's health and nutrition policies. One can only imagine the kind of research needed to develop policies on health for a candy company.

Michael R. Taylor, Deputy Commissioner of Foods at the USDA. Taylor spent more than ten years representing Monsanto for the law firm King & Spaulding. I wonder how this experience helps shape his job as a senior food safety advisor.

Roger Beachy, former head of the National Institute of Food and Agriculture. For two years he oversaw billions of dollars of competitive grants given out by the USDA. This position was only recently created and doesn't require congressional approval, and he was the first to hold it. He was the founding president of Monsanto's nonprofit research organization the Danforth Science Center, served for ten years before stepping down, and remained on the board while head of the NIFA. He is back at the Danforth Center as of this writing.

Ann Veneman, former Secretary of Agriculture. She was on the board of directors at Calgene, the first company to successfully create and market a GMO crop, Flavr Savr tomatoes. She also became the adversary of organic farmer Arthur Harvey who sued the USDA and was the defendant in the case *Harvey vs. Veneman*.

Matt Paul, Director of Communications at the USDA. He was brought in when Tom Vilsack became head of the USDA because he had been Vilsack's political public relations guy for the last decade.

Ramona Romero, Chief Legal Counsel at the USDA. She also happened to be a former corporate counsel to DuPont for twelve years.

This is not to say that there aren't many good people at the USDA looking out for our interests. There was J. Dudley Butler, who looked out for the little farmers before he quit due to political pressure against his efforts. Kathleen Merrigan, the deputy secretary, is an organic food expert. Dr. Robert Kremer is a USDA research scientist who reports unbiased findings about pesticides. These people do their best to bring integrity to a broken system, often under great duress. Their job is made much more difficult by the many colleagues who collect two paychecks. What is interesting is that none of the people who have a history of corporate involvement hold lower level positions. All of them hold either chief or director roles and make the managing decisions for many key areas of food policy. Not only do these people have the power to affect the American food supply, but their decisions influence other countries, as well. Canada toes the line when it comes to food regulations created by the United States.

In January 2011, plant pathologist and professor emeritus Dr. Don Huber at Purdue University wrote a letter to Secretary of Agriculture Tom Vilsack. In it he warned that he had discovered a highly dangerous pathogen connected to using Round-Up, which came to his attention as part of his work with the American Phytopathological Society committee on Emerging Diseases and Pathogens. This committee works for the USDA National Plant Disease Recovery System. He warned that the pathogen was found most often in corn and soybeans and had been found in the livestock that eat them with devastating consequences. It was causing pigs and cows to become infertile and suffer spontaneous abortions.

"I believe the threat we are facing from this pathogen is unique and of a high risk status. In layman's terms, it should be treated as an emergency," he said. He added that the threat to humans could be very real. The USDA and EPA made no immediate response to this letter, but Monsanto denied that anything of that nature could be possible. Less than a month later, the USDA approved Round-Up Ready alfalfa and deregulated Round-Up Ready sugar beets.

Huber sent a follow-up letter to the European Commission the next month, writing, "Based on the scientific evidence currently accumulating, I do not believe it is in the best interests of the agricultural producer or consuming public for regulatory agencies to approve more GMO crops, particularly Round-Up Ready alfalfa and sugar beets, until independent research can establish their productivity when predisposed to potentially severe diseases, the irrelevance of the new EM [electron microscope] organism, and their nutritional equivalency." The scientists didn't have a name for the new organism, simply calling it after the equipment needed to see it.

It is really no surprise that despite top researchers' warnings, the USDA continues to deregulate GMOs and promote the use of glyphosate. Tom Vilsack finally wrote his own public statement concerning the approval of Round-Up Ready alfalfa:

> These actions have generated tremendous interest in USDA's and my intentions regarding our ability to objectively regulate GE [genetically engineered] agricultural products and whether we are focused enough on science. I have tremendous confidence in our existing regulatory system and no doubts about the safety of the products this system has approved and will continue to approve. . . . The rapid adoption of GE crops has clashed with the rapid expansion of demand for organic and other non-GE products. This clash led to litigation and uncertainty.

After outlining the problems, he highlighted his strategy: "By continuing to bring stakeholders together in an attempt to find common ground where the balanced interests of all sides could be advanced, we at USDA are striving to lead an effort to forge a new paradigm based on coexistence and cooperation."

Vilsack's statement is a warning that Round-Up Ready crops will continue to be approved and no court case is going to stop that.

Monsanto Public Relations

"We will depend on them for every seed we grow, every crop we grow, and if they control seed they control food, they know it. It's strategic. It's more powerful than bombs, it's more powerful than guns."

—Vandana Shiva, environmental activist,
The World According to Monsanto documentary

Monsanto's public relations department is extremely aggressive. Besides launching large-scale marketing campaigns, the department is known to go after anything or anyone that puts the company in a negative light. I had experience with this firsthand when I published an article on my website in which I analyzed the Svalbard Global Seed Vault and who had invested in it. The vault is a highly secure seed bank located inside a mountain in Norway, created to form a safe treasure of agricultural seeds. My conclusion was that Monsanto invested heavily in the project through The Global Crop Diversity Trust, a nonprofit organization that has some control over the design and fate of the vault, and was listed on the website as a donor along with Syngenta and DuPont, as many news articles have confirmed.

Imagine my surprise when I got a comment from an anonymous person known only as "Crop" who argued lengthily about who did and did not have any ties to the seed vault. "In particular, Monsanto Corporation has had nothing at all to do with the project," this person wrote. He or she added, "No GM seeds are stored in the Seed Vault. The administration of the Seed Vault has decided against specifying which diversity is worthy of being conserved for future generations; that would be presumptuous and risky. Nevertheless, at this time, the Seed Vault does not offer storage to GM varieties." It was immediately apparent to me that this was a copy-and-paste job by some public relations intern at Monsanto. The point of my analysis was not that the seed vault would be storing GM varieties (which is not true), but whether Monsanto was allowed to have access to the vault at all. The commenter went on to say, "Only the depositor (that is, the group that sends the seeds to Svalbard) has access to the seeds. The packages and the boxes that hold them are never opened, and only the depositor can retrieve them if needed. It works like a safety-deposit box in a bank—Norway owns the Vault, and the depositor owns the seeds stored there, and is the only entity allowed to access the seeds." This isn't exactly true. It's not a safety deposit box in the strictest sense because the depositor can direct the vault to open the seeds or give them to someone else without being there. This is called a "black box arrangement" by the vault. However, the whole point of a safety-deposit box is that someone else can't even touch it, and I believe that the Svalbard Global Seed Vault does not work that way.

Every entity that makes a deposit to the seed vault must also sign a contract that grants access to their genetic material under the International Treaty on Plant Genetic Resources for Food and Agriculture. This means that all the seeds in the vault are available freely to those who are going to use the material "for research, breeding, and training for food and agriculture." This access is also completely private, without anyone keeping a record of it, as the contract states: "Access shall be accorded expeditiously, without the need to track individual accessions and free of charge."

It's interesting that Monsanto is no longer listed as a direct donor on the Diversity Fund website, although other GM companies remain on the list. Monsanto continues to be insecure about its involvement in anything to do with the vault. What we have is Syngenta, DuPont, Monsanto, and others donating millions to this seed vault and using the greatest repository of seeds in the world as a genetic base for their food and agriculture research and breeding, for free. They are desperate to keep it that way.

Even more insidious are the highly public campaigns targeting children. Monsanto has created a complete curriculum on the wonders of Bioengineering. Younger children receive happy coloring books describing the wonders of genetic engineering in simple terms, while high school students watch a video about how genetic engineering will save the poorest people from starvation and carry humanity into the future. This happens in Canada as well as the United States, and it is clear that while Monsanto may not have any hope of becoming the hero right now, it certainly hopes to for the next generation.

Although the company can't really save its own reputation completely, this attention to detail has been successful in certain aspects. Most people believe that Monsanto harassing farmers is hyperbole, despite its history, and this public perception has played an important role in recent lawsuits. For example, The Organic Seed Growers and Trade Association, made up of organic farmers and companies who make their living by avoiding GMO seeds, began a lawsuit in an effort to protect themselves from genetic drift. They wanted immunity if Monsanto discovered GM varieties in their crops, so that they could not be sued for patent infringement.

The case was quickly thrown out, with the judge asserting that the farmers' claims were exaggerated since none of them had ever been sued, and Monsanto only litigated against a relatively small number of farmers per year, a fact confirmed by Monsanto on its own website: "Since 1997, we have only filed suit against farmers 145 times in the United States. This may sound like a lot, but when you consider that we sell seed to more than 250,000 American farmers a year, it's really a small number. Of these, we've proceeded through trial with only eleven farmers. All eleven cases were found in Monsanto's favor."

If you have watched any number of popular documentaries (such as *The World According to Monsanto* or *Food, Inc.*), you have probably seen several farmers claiming that Monsanto employees had trespassed on their properties looking for proof that the farmers had been saving seeds illegally. Monsanto executives claim that they have only done this in extreme situations and only if there is clear proof that the farmer has intentionally saved a massive quantity of patented seed. Monsanto claims it would never sue someone for genetic drift, which only contaminates a small proportion of a field, and that it would only take action if a farmer actively saved seeds for planting the next year, instead of buying them again from Monsanto. While it is difficult to extrapolate the real story when both sides are so biased, from Monsanto's own account we can get a fairly clear picture of what is going on.

There are two cases of particular interest. The first involves Gary Rinehart, owner of the Square Deal general store in Eagleville, Missouri. Eagleville has a population of 314 and everyone knows everyone else, especially the owner of the only store. It was a typical day and the store had a few customers in it, when anonymous "investigators" approached Gary. Without introduction, these investigators made a public accusation that Gary was stealing Monsanto intellectual property by planting and saving patented seed. These representatives were shocked when "he became angry, attracting the attention of others in the store, prompting Monsanto's representatives to leave. They were there for less than two minutes" (Monsanto). It was a puzzling accusation since Gary was not a farmer and hadn't planted anything. It turned out that the actual person Monsanto needed to talk to was Gary's son Tim, who had planted patented seeds at some point (although there doesn't seem to be any proof of theft). Monsanto claims that they reached a settlement with Tim, but Tim has never paid.

The second case was with farmer Dave Runyon, producer of corn, wheat, and soybeans in Indiana. He admitted that he grew GM corn, but had never purchased the seed from Monsanto, a fact that Monsanto should have known from their customer database. He is one of the rare farmers who grow regular old wheat and soybeans. The "investigators" approached

Dave in 2005 on his property, accusing him of growing Monsanto soybeans. They demanded production records, but Dave refused to provide proof that he was not stealing GM soybeans, and so Monsanto made the decision to blacklist him from ever purchasing any Monsanto products in the future, which he was fine with since he never had in the first place. Runyon claims that Monsanto followed up with a letter claiming that they had an agreement with the Indiana Department of Agriculture for him to turn over his production records to them, but at that time there was no Department of Agriculture in Indiana.

In any other kind of business, if men arrive on your property unannounced, asking for proof that you aren't stealing from them, you would most likely be a victim of organized crime. Neither Runyon nor Rinehart had ever been a Monsanto customer, yet Monsanto was investigating them for crimes and personally confronting them. Monsanto spokespeople tell these stories themselves arguing that it only happens "rarely." But should it even happen at all?

The Organic Seed Growers and Trade Association (OSGATA) had higher hopes for their trial to protect themselves against situations like these, but at least theirs is a step in the right direction. They have now filed an appeal that has even greater public support than before. Unfortunately they can't sue Monsanto for genetic drift because that is a much more difficult case. Jim Gerritsen, President of OSGATA stated,

> Monsanto's threats and abuse of family farmers stops here. Monsanto's genetic contamination of organic seed and organic crops ends now. Americans have the right to choice in the marketplace—to decide what kind of food they will feed their families. . . . Organic farmers have the right to raise our organic crops for our families and our customers on our farms without the threat of invasion by Monsanto's genetic contamination and without harassment by a reckless polluter.

As the pressure grows, Monsanto is known to become more and more public with its bullying. Monsanto is headed by some of the world's most powerful and politically-connected people, and it has a lot of money tied up in food. Controlling it is their business. When the Vermont legislature was poised to pass a popular and groundbreaking bill in April 2012 that would require labeling on all GM foods, which fifty countries already require, Monsanto threatened to sue the state if the bill was passed. Bill H.722 was simply following in the footsteps of most of the world's developed nations. Unfortunately, thanks to Monsanto, the bill remained dead in the water for 2012.

Saving Seed

"Though I do not believe that a plant will spring up where no seed has been, I have great faith in a seed. Convince me that you have a seed there, and I am prepared to expect wonders."

—Henry David Thoreau

If you haven't figured it out already, seeds are pretty important. Each tiny seed carries thousands of years of evolutionary history, waiting until just the right moment to burst into life. Within a few days, a dormant little speck no bigger than a grain of sand becomes a white sprout stretching up towards the light, and only weeks later is a tall green ready to be eaten. Each variety carries the potential of continuing the species despite predators, weather, and disease, and each species could be the possible salvation of some human society facing starvation.

It is also very clear that this diversity is under threat. We have fewer farmers; most of the food we eat comes from a few seeds created by a few corporations; the plants are totally dependent on man-made products to survive; and political battles are waging over what we can and can't control. We are putting ourselves in a precarious position.

The solution is to save seed. There are many small companies and non-profit organizations that are preserving heirloom varieties. The first step is acquiring these and growing them yourself by getting in contact with Seed Savers Exchange, Seeds of Diversity, or other preservation groups. Not only do these growers offer organic heirloom seeds, they also have many educational resources on how to preserve seeds. There's really no excuse for not saving seeds—even urban dwellers growing things in containers can do it.

A Little Science

All right, I admit that it's not quite as simple as I made it sound. Just like our interaction with the soil, interacting with plants requires a little knowledge of science, or, if you prefer, intuitive knowledge of the magical forces of nature. To make seeds, plants must *flower*. It takes male and female flower parts to make a seed, and for some species these are on the same plant. Others have male and female parts on separate plants. The pollen from the male part must make it to the female part and thus seeds are born.

For serious seed savers, your first concern is to make sure your pollen isn't contaminated by another variety. This is the big problem with GM genetic drift. The pollen containing all that genetic material mixes up the DNA of your own strain, creating something else entirely. You'll have to have a basic understanding of how your particular plant gets pollinated and how to keep it isolated. The wind and bees are the biggest culprits in contamination.

1. Only grow one variety of the species you want to save.
2. Bear in mind the distance between you and other gardens. Is your neighbor growing carrots? Each variety has an optimum isolation distance, which is information you can find out from any of the resources listed in the back of this book. If this is not possible, plant earlier or later than your neighbor so that your plants flower at different times.
3. You can only save seeds from open-pollinated varieties, which is usually indicated on the packet if you purchase it from a good source.

Hybrids (or F1 hybrids), will produce seeds that are not *true to type*, that is, the child of a plant grown from a hybrid seed may not look anything like its parent. This is because they are like clones and genetically identical, and if they have children they will all be inbred and look like the grandparent plants. Open-pollinated varieties will carry the traits of the parent plants, although there may be a lot of variation. There's nothing wrong with hybrids, it's just difficult to breed them.

4. You can isolate the flowers of a plant by covering them in bags made out of mesh or paper, but this is not preferable. The bags can get in the way once you start pollinating, and they can increase the chances of mold or wilt or other problems. The simplest way to ensure pollination is to do so by hand, literally. Use your finger or a paintbrush and mimic the actions of a bee. It may seem like a lot of trouble, but each plant will produce thousands of seeds and careful pollination ensures that your plants stay pure.

Once you are well on your way to serious seed saving, you'll learn how to *rogue out*. Rogueing out just means saving only the seeds from plants that are true to type, that carry the traits of the parents. This takes some practice, but is the most important part of saving good seed. If a carrot variety grows long, has a bright white root, and is resistant to carrot fly, then you would certainly not save seed from a short, orange carrot that was injured by carrot flies. Sometimes the discrepancies are more subtle; you may decide not to save the seed of the tomato that was less red, or even less sweet.

When your true-to-type plant successfully makes seeds that have been appropriately isolated from contamination from other varieties, it's time to save them. Gather the seeds and lay them out to dry. For some seeds, you'll have to first remove any pulp and wash them off. Although some people use a dehydrator, heat is a bad thing because high temperatures can either kill the seed or make it germinate early. It works just as well to lay them out on a surface that is low in humidity. A large board, screen, or pan is ideal. Paper and cloth will stick to the seeds, so keep the surface bare. A gentle fan to keep air circulating in the room (but not blow directly on the seeds) can help speed the process, which generally takes a couple of days to a week.

Once dry, the seeds should last about a year if stored properly. Put them in a clean, dry container. It does not have to be airtight. In fact, sealing too tightly can increase the chances of mold. If you plan to use the seeds within a few months, store them in a cool, dry, and dark location. If you need to store them longer than that, put them in the refrigerator.

Now you can feel proud that not only did you save some money, but you also have prevented thousands of years of hard work from going to waste, saved a species from disappearing, and stuck it to Monsanto.

CHAPTER THREE

A Vast Desert

"The factory farm has succeeded by divorcing people from their food, eliminating farmers, and ruling agriculture by corporate fiat."

—Jonathan Safran Foer, *Eating Animals*

Food Deserts

"The day is coming when a single carrot, freshly observed, will set off a revolution."

—Paul Cezanne

The phrase *food desert* is a helpfully graphic term describing a place where people have very limited or no access to grocery stores that carry fresh food. In lower-income urban neighborhoods, not everyone has a vehicle, so food must be located within walking distance or a bus ride away. Larger grocery stores tend to place themselves in affluent suburbs because it's more profitable, leaving the corner store, gas station, and convenience stores to fill in the gaps. It's a vicious cycle: On a continuous quest to buy food, a family must choose whatever will fill them up most effectively and give them enough energy to sustain their activity. Fresh vegetables are expensive, and you have to eat more of them to meet daily caloric requirements. They are even more expensive at convenience stores, if they have fresh food at all. Many families end up buying processed meats, canned goods, and packaged foods, because they're easy to get and carry home. Unfortunately, these kinds of foods lead to health problems like obesity and cancer.

The definition of a food desert usually only applies to people far below the poverty line. With enough money, a family can get fresh food no matter how far away the grocery store is. However, most studies on food deserts consider vegetables in the grocery store to be fresh, but that is not always the case.

According to a 2009 study in the *HortScience*, vegetables at the grocery store have 5 to 40 percent less minerals than ones eaten fifty years ago. Vegetables are forced to grow larger and faster, but that doesn't actually increase their nutritional value. A larger pepper or tomato doesn't have more minerals, just more dry matter with lower concentrations of vitamins. An early harvest also means that the plant didn't have as much time to absorb minerals from the soil, and from farms using chemical fertilizer, there aren't many minerals anyway.

Add to this the incredible length of time food is in storage before it hits your plate and it becomes questionable what a grocery store vegetable actually does for the human body. Lettuce is kept in storage for four to ten days and tomatoes for at least a week. Baby carrots wait two to three weeks to get to the store, while larger carrots don't make it there for six months. According to a 2003 issue of *The Observer*, apples and potatoes spend six to twelve months in storage. All these fruits and vegetables will probably spend additional time in your refrigerator and lose even more nutritional value before you finally eat them.

The truth of the matter is that as soon as a vegetable or fruit is picked, it is no longer alive and its cells begin to break down. Food that has been harvested from the ground in less than twenty-four hours is difficult to find, even for affluent people. There aren't enough farms selling within that twenty-four-hour time frame. This is true for every region in North America. According to the USDA statistics, small farms only produce 5 percent or less of the vegetables in any given area.

Local farms work on timetables, with food available only during a limited season, and also only available during certain days of the week. All of these limitations serve to drive up prices. Often the cost is not based on the high price of production, but rather the availability of the product. Truly fresh food is most often only available to people who have the time to visit local farms and the money to pay the higher prices. These are the people who are keeping the local food movement alive today, but this scenario means that just 15 percent of Americans are getting local food.

The path from farm to consumer is called a *foodshed*, and there is no town in North America that has successfully created a foodshed, where everyone has access to affordable, locally grown fresh food, even during the summer. There are many cities and community groups that are trying, but like any government initiative, it takes much too long. Families do not want to wait years for the completion of a feasibility study while they wait for fresh food to become available. Unfortunately, grassroots projects often take longer because of lack of funding.

By contrast, France has never lost its access to good food. The French people demand quality and they were early adopters of the community farm model, similar to Community Supported Agriculture (CSA), through their Associations for the Maintenances of Smallholder Agriculture. France is *food sovereign*, or has the ability to feed all of its population with food grown within France. The French *"Appellation d'origine contrôlée"* label (AOC), loosely translated as "Controlled designation of origin," guarantees a product's origin under the concept of *terroir*. *Terroir* comes from the word *terre*, or land, and denotes foods that are unique to a region, and the soil of a special place. It is based on the idea that no matter how hard you try to reproduce the conditions and techniques of a particular food, you can never do it unless you are in that specific location. This began particularly for wine, but has extended to other foods, as well. The AOC label is controversial because it is illegal to label a product even with a regional name unless it has been produced under defined standards, and the standards can sometimes be fuzzy and philosophical. But it does do the important job of putting a value and a standard on local labeling.

This kind of local labeling legislation has been fought fiercely in the United States, and in places without regulation the end result is food labeling that is haphazard and inaccurate. Grocery stores often label a food as coming from California, when it was only packaged there and grown in Mexico or Peru. A study in the United Kingdom by the government watchdog LGR (Local Government Regulation) found that 18 percent of food labels about location were absolutely false, and another 14 percent could not be verified. To be labeled as local according to regulation, food must have come from within 30 miles (50 km) away. This means that one-third of all local food is not really local. Before we place blame, however, keep in mind that 15 percent of people are trying to get a small portion of available produce. If the demand is too high, the pressure is that much greater to satisfy the customer. Is there a place anywhere that is even close to solving these problems?

A group of people in the town of Todmorden in West Yorkshire, England, began in 2008 with a ten-year vision to grow enough food for their 17,000 residents. They started with the simple idea to transform the source of their town's food by growing it all locally in whatever space was available by 2018. Incredible Edible Todmorden, which is what they called their initiative, had no funding sources and no government sup-port, but they knew they wanted to begin without waiting for permission. An herb garden was expanded to include vegetables, orchards, chickens, and massive school programs. Eventually they did capture the support of the local government by approaching the town for land after they had filled all the other available space. What began as a food desert has become an oasis. A surprising benefit has been the lower crime rate and the improvement to the community, bringing together people of all ages and creating a sense of purpose where there wasn't one before. The police found that in the second year there were 259 fewer crimes than the year before, and as local sergeant Michael Bowden said, "The cynics have been proved wrong. Crime has gone down because everyone has ownership of the land" (Geographical). It is doubtful, however, that Todmorden will become food sovereign by 2018. The task is just too big, even with its small population.

Grocery Stores and Middlemen

"Anyone who believes the competitive spirit in America is dead has never been in a supermarket when the cashier opens another checkout line."

—Ann Landers

The first grocery stores in North America were general or dry goods stores. They rarely offered fresh food. Instead they sold things that people couldn't grow or make themselves and things that could be stored away for months at a time, such as canned goods, flour, and sugar. During that time, you walked directly up to the counter and told the owner or clerk exactly what you wanted, and he would bring it to you. He would tell you the price, and you could possibly haggle over it, and then you paid cash or bartered something of your own. It wasn't until Piggly Wiggly was founded in 1916 that this changed. It all began with the novel idea that shoppers could simply grab things off the shelf for themselves.

Piggly Wiggly invented many revolutionary changes, but the biggest one was the ability to buy in high volume and offer lower prices to customers. Having the ability to buy products for hundreds of stores rather than just one gave it negotiating power that no one else had. No longer would there be haggling or time-consuming debates with customers over prices. The industry immediately latched onto this and grocery store chains began popping up everywhere in the 1920s. Soon there were tens of thousands of them across America. By 1940 all these little stores had conglomerated and created *supermarkets*, with butchers, bakers, produce managers, and dry goods all under one roof. By the 1950s these supermarkets had already migrated to the suburbs, leaving the little corner groceries in the dust. It only took thirty years before the general store had disappeared.

In the process of relocating the small store to the supermarket, and the urban to the suburban, the way food was distributed changed, as well. Almost all farmers at the turn of the century sold directly to the customer or to a produce man who sold directly to customers. There was never more than one middleman. When grocery stores became larger and larger and farms became distanced from the population, food distribution became much more complex. Here's how it works: The farmer sells to food wholesalers through a broker. The broker negotiates a deal between the wholesaler and farmer, taking a cut in the process. The wholesaler then sells the food at a marked-up price to the grocery chain in large quantities. This food is then trucked to a warehouse where it sits for a week until it can be placed on a shelf in a store.

Then there are *marketing boards*. In the United States, the boards are organizations that farmers can voluntarily belong to and act as policy watchdogs and advertising representatives. Although they really only represent factory farms, they serve the interests of farmers who pay a rate to the board based on how much they produce. The farmers make the choice to pay this fee because it provides ensurance that they will continue to receive government subsidies and retain control of their distribution system. In Canada, however, these boards are much more insidious. If the farmer produces a "regulated" product, he must then comply with whatever policy the board decides. These Canadian boards have the ultimate power to fix prices, require farmers to sell through certain distributors rather than directly to customers, and help manage subsidies. To sell a regulated product on more than a backyard scale, the farmer must purchase a quota on a unit price. Today, there are no quotas left because they were bought up years ago and they are inheritable, and the boards don't create more. These boards have completely locked up production of most food staples in Canada, including cabbage, potatoes, carrots, milk, greenhouse tomatoes, wheat, and more. It is impossible for young farmers to break in. If you choose to grow and sell a regulated product without a quota, these boards have the right to seize your property, levy ridiculous fines, and even send you to jail.

We've looked at how farmers, brokers, distributors, marketing boards, and stores participate in this process. Now add to this the lobbyists and government agricultural departments working to manipulate prices, plan subsidies, and create multimillion-dollar marketing campaigns aimed at consumers. All of these actors need to be paid, and the people at both ends of this chain are the ones who pay for it: the farmer and the consumer.

Imagine you are a potato farmer with 100 acres of potatoes. Your farm is worth about $2 million because of the arable land and the $600,000 worth of large potato harvesting equipment you own. It costs about $2,300 per acre to produce the potatoes, which is what it takes to operate the huge machinery and pay for the pesticides that resist blight. The wholesale price is about $10 per hundredweight, and each acre brings in $2,750 per acre. This is a profit of $450 per acre, from which you must then pay your hired farm labor and yourself. This $45,000 is not very much to split between the several families needed to bring in the harvest.

The broker, who usually specializes in just potatoes, negotiated the wholesale price of $10. Most of the time the farmer also has to pay him a brokerage fee for the service of finding someone to buy the potatoes. Usually this buyer is a distributor who might also specialize in potatoes. This distributor sorts through the potatoes looking for blemishes, packages them, and finds a buyer who wants to sell them. If they can't find an immediate buyer, they store the potatoes in long-term storage. The buyer could be a grocery store if they are Grade A potatoes, or it could be a food processing company that makes french fries and potato chips. Those potatoes would go to a factory for chopping and dipping in various mixtures before being packaged and finally ending up at a fast food chain or grocery store. The final buyer, the consumer, has to pay all the people who touched the potatoes after they left the farm, and that's what determines the retail price. Brokers will try to push down the wholesale price for the farmer and increase the retail price for the consumer.

Food prices rose drastically as the recession began to build momentum in 2011. People assume this is because of "the economy," or climate change and bad weather, but this is only partly true. Raw goods in their most basic form are called *commodities*, and when people hear that word they usually think of things like copper or coal. But one major commodity you don't hear much about is food. During the last decade, investment banks like Goldman Sachs had begun helping investors *speculate* on food crops. Speculation is the exact opposite of an investment, which usually has a fairly guaranteed return. Speculation is risky, lacking any research or backing that would ensure that you would get your money back, but sometimes it has big financial returns. It is exactly like gambling, but with the world's food supply in this case.

When speculators bet on *futures* of corn and soybeans, they pay a price for a future crop of food and hope that in the end it sells for more than they paid. Previously, future trading was a way of stabilizing the market. Farmers would make a deal to sell future crops for a specific price, which gave them some insurance and predictability. However, when this system was deregulated, the speculators were able to cause problems by manipulating it in ways that drove up prices instead of stabilizing them. The price is created in the moment by looking at what people paid for it in the past, and if people in the past pay more and more through speculation, the price goes up. This also increases the likelihood of hoarding. If prices are low, wheat dealers can store grain away until prices go up, and they can see what will happen in the future based on the price of grain futures.

If you think it sounds complex, it is, and my description is incredibly rudimentary compared to the actual process. It could not be more remote from the dry goods stores of the last century. Within a hundred years, humans have taken something as simple as food and turned it into a billion-dollar machine with many moving parts. Who knows, really, what the results would be if the machine came to a grinding halt? The food system hangs in a fragile balance, and yet is made up of a large army of people all trying to serve their own interests.

Right now there is plenty of food in the world to feed everyone in it, especially the starving ones. But the middlemen need to make their cut, so the farmer stays poor, the food is stockpiled, gambled on, and distributed to the wealthy in the suburbs. When people cry out that they can't afford food, these players lie, "There is a global food shortage! The world population is too high and the weather is bad and the farmers didn't grow enough." They blame the farmer for the side effects of their own game.

Not only are the wealthy and privileged of the civilized world eating more and consuming more and wasting more than any other creatures on Earth, they are also storing away food to drive up the price so others can't eat it.

Assembly Line Food Production

"As with any violent ideology, the populace must be shielded from direct exposure to the victims of the system, lest they begin questioning the system or their participation in it. This truth speaks for itself: Why else would the meat industry go to such lengths to keep its practices invisible?"
—Melanie Joy, *Why We Love Dogs, Eat Pigs, and Wear Cows*

America invented the *assembly line*—or rather, Henry Ford did—sometime around 1910 to increase the efficiency of producing the automobile. Assembly-line production is undeniably a faster and cheaper way of making things. Rather than a few people handcrafting an entire car, a line of people are each given responsibility for one part. What starts out as a pile of parts at the beginning pops out as an entire functional car at the end. This concept was pure genius and caught on all over the world. It has been applied to every industry, including food production.

We know farmers are a dying breed, but what we don't often appreciate is that *factory farming* is a major cause. This is a popular phrase right now, and the media has caught on to sensationalizing hidden camera footage of evil factory farms abusing animals, but most people don't really have an understanding of what factory farms are. A commonly held belief is that factory farms are run by corporations and exist as the evil nemesis of the good family-owned farms.

This is not really true. Most farms, even factory farms, are family-owned and have been for generations. The reason they become attached to a corporation is because of the food distribution system. The marketing board or corporation sets a limit on how much of a certain product is produced to artificially balance the market and keep prices competitive. Farms are granted quotas, or capacity, based on their size and how much the managing organization wants to produce. In Canada this quantity is set by the marketing boards that the farmer has to belong to by law, and in the United States it is set by the corporation, which has the power to quickly take away a family's livelihood. Although the two systems are different, the results are the same and there is not much the farmers can do about it. Quotas are set for egg and meat producers, as well, which is one factor contributing to the high incidence of animal abuse and neglect. When a farm has acquired a quota (a number of animals it is allowed to have), there is tremendous pressure to maintain that quota. If the farmer can't keep it up, the farm loses the quota, and it is next to impossible to get back. Without the quota, and reliable income over one season, the farm is usually lost forever. As farms become more and more conglomerated, it becomes more and more difficult to take a piece of the production supply.

How is a factory farm different?

If factory farms are just family farms that have conglomerated and were given a quota by a marketing board or corporation, then what makes the farm a factory? Activists, not farmers, coined the phrase *factory farm*. Factory farms are really known in the industry as Industrial Farm Animal Production (IFAP) or Animal Feedlot Operations (AFO). There are more than 450,000 IFAPs or AFOs in the United States, also called *feedlots*, producing 99 percent of America's meat (and 95 percent in Canada). Some of these are the bigwigs, such as Concentrated Animal Feeding Operations (CAFO), which houses 125,000 animals under one roof. In 2007 approximately 20,000 AFOs were CAFOs (Wiedeman).

North America has gotten itself into quite a fix. You can't just wish away 450,000 farms producing 99 percent of your meat, but that doesn't really excuse industrial farms. Feedlots produce unimaginable quantities of manure and urine. On a sustainable farm, the manure and urine are valuable inputs that are composted and returned to the soil. A feedlot can't do that because there's just too much waste—so much of it, in fact, that it becomes a liability rather than a resource. The waste has to be piped to a giant *lagoon* or cesspool containing millions of gallons and covering acres of land, where it festers and emits toxic gases. Sometimes the manure is sprayed onto the field without composting, which only hurts the soil and water supply by leeching nitrates and harboring dangerous bacteria and antibiotics. Working around these cesspools is unbearable, and just getting a whiff of the hydrogen sulfide they produce can cause serious health problems.

Keeping all these animals so close together causes a host of other problems. One of the first issues is an ethical one. Feedlot animals are crammed together, often without shelter, and can't move around very much. The waste is never cleaned out completely, so they wallow around in their own feces. Their water supplies and feed troughs should be cleaned daily, but this is hardly possible with farms managing tens of thousands of animals. This overcrowding and lack of hygiene obviously breeds disease, and many of the animals would be sick or dead without preventative antibiotics to keep them alive and well. Feedlot producers are also often guilty of skimping on feed and choosing the cheapest possible food for their animals. This is why cows are the largest consumers of corn, which they aren't supposed to eat but which fattens them up quickly.

Cows need protein, which large feedlots supply with soybeans or *bone meal*. Bone meal is the ground up and cooked parts of other animals, usually from the waste of slaughtering or from sick cows that have been put down. It is much cheaper in Europe to get bone meal than soy, and in the United Kingdom there was a sudden repercussion. By 2009 mad cow disease had killed 210 people, almost all of them because they had eaten British meat. By 2011 another 22 people had died, including several in Canada and in the United States from American and Canadian beef. While it is known that bone meal from infected animals spreads the disease, the actual cause of the disease is still unknown. Government authorities dispute the claim that new rules allowing bone meal to be processed at a lower temperature had anything to do with it. Various steps were taken to prevent an outbreak from happening again, but the fact remains that feedlots do not make decisions based on the health of animals or even people. It's all about the bottom line. Government regulation fell short and has continued to fail to protect consumers over and over again, especially since mad cow is a completely preventable disease. When large-scale farmers make so little profit on each cow, they feel tremendous pressure to reduce costs. Even those with tens of thousands of animals may be living on the edge of bankruptcy because of insurmountable debt.

After the mad cow scare, the US government required rigorous testing on cows, sampling almost 400,000 cows every year. They found that the incidence of mad cow in the United States is extremely rare, affecting one in a million cows, and they only found one case. However, they only test dead cows, not live animals displaying strange behavior. Because of their findings, the USDA decided to cut back on testing and now only samples 40,000 cows, or 0.1 percent of cattle, each year.

However, in April 2012, a dairy cow in California was discovered with an atypical strain. The USDA has said that such rare cases happen spontaneously, which stops authorities from being able to prevent illness through screening, but this statement contradicts everything we know about mad cow disease. It is clearly transmitted through feed and not some spontaneous occurrence. This Californian cow had BASE (bovine amyloidotic spongiform encephalopathy) or L-type atypical BSE. Typical BSE is the British version, and it caused cows to get more aggressive and twitchy while their brains developed holes like Swiss cheese. It was easy to recognize a sick cow just by looking at it. The atypical American version makes the cows weak and unable to stand up, a common occurrence in the cow world. Cows are subject to a variety of illnesses causing weakness, so eyeballing the cattle is an unreliable screening method. These *downer cows* are slaughtered and sent straight into our food supply, a risk that the USDA is willing to take. Unfortunately this atypical strain has higher transmissibility and is more fatal to animals and humans.

Allegations against factory farms for animal rights violations usually come from undercover activists with hidden cameras, as in the case of the turkey farm in North Carolina that supplied birds to Butterball. Mercy for Animals managed to get an activist with a hidden camera a job at the facility. Once several weeks of footage were collected, the organization blew the whistle, which resulted in a search by government authorities in 2011. The video included disturbing and violent footage of complacent, but obviously unhealthy birds being kicked, poked, thrown, and dragged by the neck. Similar videos the same year exposed workers at farms that supplied beef, pork, and eggs to Costco and McDonald's throwing, burning, and suffocating animals and even beating young calves to death. It is clear from these videos that government inspections are doing little to prevent not just animal cruelty, but also adequate hygiene. Animals in the videos are emaciated and covered in sores from standing still in their own feces for much too long, and decomposed birds are left in cages next to live ones laying eggs for human consumption.

These conditions build up over time and eventually end up in people's mouths. Once these animals go to slaughter, the meat or eggs are mixed together through the mass distribution system, and the origins become untraceable. For example, at the end of 2011, Hannaford Supermarkets enacted a voluntary recall of all ground beef sold in their stores over a thirty-seven-day period because it was contaminated with *Salmonella typhimurium* strain (Gaffney, USDA). Ten people became ill, which doesn't seem like a high number compared to the amount of beef that was sold, but it was a very dangerous outbreak because it was aggressive and resistant to antibiotics. Each salmonella outbreak in the United States can usually be traced to a source because it has its own identifiable DNA code, and this one was rare and unique, which meant that the Centers for Disease Control and Prevention could not trace the source of the meat to any particular area. The Food Safety department of the USDA recommended that consumers always prepare their own beef, hinting that the contaminated beef had probably spread to more outlets than just Hannaford Supermarkets.

The factory farm moniker isn't usually applied to field crops because you can't abuse a vegetable, but I would argue that most big industrialized monoculture farms are factory farms, as well. They are hundreds of acres in size and use massive machinery to till the soil and harvest food, functioning as a factory in every sense of the word. These farms have many of the same health problems as feedlots because they use raw fertilizers and chemicals, which hurt not only the people using them, but also the surrounding community. Perhaps monoculture can grow certain crops more efficiently, but it's a trap in the long run. Growing one thing over and over attracts pests and diseases, which in turn require more chemicals. As more chemicals are used, pests and diseases become more resistant. It is a never-ending vicious cycle with terrible costs, as Rachel Carson predicted fifty years ago in *Silent Spring.* Despite her early prophecy, we have been slow to react, and the damage is already done.

It's not a problem that can just go away, and change is very slow. People have become aware that most of their food comes from factory farms, but there is still an attitude of acceptance. In 2004, Organic Valley, a cooperative of small family farms, ordered a survey from independent research firm Roper Public Affairs to find out who Americans trusted. The survey found that 7 out of 10 people trust industrial and factory farms to produce safe, nutritious food, but at the same time, 7 out of 10 people believe that small farms care more about food safety. This apparent conflict in beliefs has a lot to do with the American diet, which most people don't want to change.

Seventy-three percent of people believe that buying local food is important, but at the same time they have become victims of powerful marketing. They have been told that organic and local is much more expensive, that it is a short-lived fad, and that it is more trouble than it's worth. They have been told that factory farm foods are safe, and when they go to the store there is every kind of processed convenience food to choose from. It comes down to a difficult decision. People have to cook from scratch, avoid fast food, and cut back on the tremendous amount of meat that they consume. This is not so easy.

The USDA is not helping the small farms that have a clean record. Their goal seems to be to protect the big farms from too much fallout when they sell contaminated food. In fact, in 2004, Creekstone Farms Premium Beef decided to test all 300,000 of their cattle for BSE because Japan's ban on American beef for the last couple of years had forced them to lay off 150 employees. They built a testing facility and hired the necessary staff to increase customer confidence, but when it came time to purchase the BSE testing kits from the USDA or a licensed distributor, the USDA said no. The government refused to allow them to purchase the kits, telling them that testing has "no food safety value" and is "likely to produce false negative results" (Frye). This right to control testing was upheld in civil court. It seems as though even ethical factory farms aren't allowed to grow safe meat because it makes everyone else look bad.

Somewhat ironically, in 2011 Creekstone recalled 14,000 pounds of ground beef for E. coli contamination.

The Farmer's Slippery Ethical Slope

"As far as food is concerned, the great extravagance is not caviar or truffles, but beef, pork and poultry. . . . The combined weight of the world's 1.28 billion cattle alone exceeds that of the human population. While we look darkly at the number of babies being born in poorer parts of the world, we ignore the over-population of farm animals, to which we ourselves contribute."

—Peter Singer

How did the situation get so bad? We often blame the farmer or the corporation, but they are not entirely at fault. The aging farmer, struggling to hold on to land that has been farmed for hundreds of years, sometimes by his own forebears, often feels despair and heartbreak. Farmers have cash flow problems. Money comes in at the end of the year when the crops are ripe or the cows get fat, but until then, how do farmers eat and pay the bills? A farmer can feed his children if the previous year was a good one, but the income is often not quite enough to run a farm business and live on. The profit made by an industrial farm is pitifully low considering the operating costs. So the farmer sometimes has to cut corners to survive. In a matter of survival, the welfare of farm workers and animals comes second. Most farm workers are migrants and are paid very little. There is no farmer that starts out by borrowing hundreds of thousands of dollars for state-of-the-art equipment and then looks into the future to say, "Someday my barns and fields will be full of filth, and we won't be able to afford proper butchering methods so we'll beat the animals to death."

The marketing boards and corporations are often made of former farmers, but these organizations have their own agendas. They lobby with the government, and they push around millions of dollars. They offer farmers security by prepaying them for upcoming crops, giving them crop insurance in case of disaster, and providing subsidies for farmers growing certain crops. Many farmers can't afford to operate without help, and this gives those companies and boards a tremendous amount of power. However, even though they are a little too involved in politics, the marketing boards and food corporations really do keep many family farms afloat. They deal with marketing and distribution, and they make sure farmers have a reliable income and can survive if something goes wrong.

The big farms don't like the little farms. They deal out quotas or control policy to control the supply of commodities. Controlling the supply gives them tight direction over the price, and farmers who fall outside the conventional realm, such as organic or free-range growers, get the short end of the stick. For example, in British Columbia, the supply of organic and free-range eggs is not enough to meet the enormous demand. There are many small egg producers ready to step in and supply the eggs, but the BC Egg Marketing Board has created regulation that defines anyone with more than 99 chickens as a commercial producer. If you have between 100 and 399 hens and you want to sell sustainable eggs, you must enter a lottery. How this lottery program is run is sketchy at best. In 2009, only twenty small farms won the right to have under 399 chickens in all of British Columbia out of the hundreds that applied. The total number of birds equals far less than the 18,000 hens owned by a single average industrial egg farm. It is obvious that this rule has more to do with restricting competition than it does with any kind of health issue.

In the case of the egg industry, the board is made of people who hold a stake in high-tech chicken breeding and patents, such as companies like Hy-Line, which have their own molecular genetics team working towards the perfect industrial laying hen. Corporations such as Hy-Line really don't seem to care about the birds or sustainable growing practices or quotas. They just want the hamburger or eggs or potatoes delivered on time at the price they agreed on. They are retail establishments like restaurants and stores, and they are brands like Tyson and Cargill, the largest poultry companies in the United States.

Corporate brands sign contracts directly with farmers, and the farmer is then required to foot the bill for equipment and buildings to follow the procedures that the corporation stipulates. Once the farmer does so, there's no going back. Most poultry is produced in the rural South and farmed in the poorest areas of America. In a desperate attempt to save generational farmland, farmers sign away their souls to corporations and fall into millions of dollars of debt. Banks have been more than willing to lend money to poultry farmers, unfortunately. The corporation delivers the birds (genetically owned by companies like Hy-Line), the farmer raises them in the way dictated by the company, and then the corporation comes to get them for slaughter. At no point does the farmer have any decision-making capacity, and if the farmer complains, the next order for chickens just doesn't arrive. Many farmers have health problems due to the unhealthy conditions of their barns, but don't have any power to do anything about it and often can't even afford health insurance. Meanwhile, they are paid so little for each chicken that they live below the poverty line, with no hope of ever getting out of debt.

But are the corporations entirely to blame? Their business is to make money, and they produce a product that people are willing to pay for. This means keeping overhead costs low and selling high, but they are not forcing people to keep them in business. As long as people pay for Tyson chicken and KFC, there will still be factory farms and farmers living in poverty.

People don't make as much as they used to in the 1950s because living costs have gone up more than income has. We spent more on food in the '50s because our other expenses were much lower. The hourly minimum wage was about $1.50 and eggs were $0.60 per dozen. Families spent about 29 percent of their income on food, more than any other category of spending, seconded only by housing at less than 28 percent. By 1997 the percentage spent on food had dropped to 7 percent, but housing costs had gone up. According to the National Association of Realtors, in 1997 people were spending 30 to 40 percent of their income on shelter. The drop in food spending from 29 percent to 7 percent (a 22 percent difference) has created a demand for cheap food.

Small Farms Are an Endangered Species

"Burn down your cities and leave our farms, and your cities will spring up again as if by magic; but destroy our farms and the grass will grow in the streets of every city in the country."
—William Jennings Bryan, nineteenth century American politician

The US government defines a farm as any establishment that produces at least $1,000 worth of agricultural products a year. About 1 percent of Americans claim farming as a career, almost a million people, and while that number may seem like a lot, it's not. In addition, these million people are not very economically stable. The living expenses of the average farm family are more than $47,000 per year, but less than 1 in 4 farmers makes that much. This is because a very small group of farmers is making most of the sales. Of the millions of farmers selling products, 9 percent produce 63 percent of the *value*, or the total value of all the crops grown (USDA 2007 Census). The 9 percent producing all that value are defined as "large" family farms with sales over $250,000 per year, which means that the USDA measures farm size not with physical size, but with money, and defines "small" farms as those that make less than $250,000. It also means that 37 percent of all the farm value produced in 2007 came from what they define as small farms, which seems like quite a bit, but it does not measure farm growth accurately.

The USDA decreed that in 2007 there were 18,000 *more* small farms than there had been in 2002. Ninety-one percent of farms are considered small, and they call this "small farm growth," but, it's more likely that in 2007, there were 18,000 existing farms that had made less money and could no longer be called "large farms."

A more accurate way to measure small farm growth is by the age of the farm operation, and surprisingly, its actual size. In 1982 almost 40 percent of farmers had been on their current property for less than ten years, but by 2007 this was down 10 percent, while at the same time farmers who had been on their current property for more than ten years grew by 10 percent.

This only proves that the farmers who started late in the 1970s and early '80s are probably still farming today twenty-five years later, but people today aren't starting new farms as often and can't claim farming as a career. Eighty percent of those who do start farms work off the farm to pay for it, up 20 percent from 1998.

In the 1980s, the average startup farm began with 490 acres. Today, the average startup farm begins with 200 and is less likely to be profitable. Before 1998 more than 50 percent of small farms made a positive net income, but today that is down to 33 percent. Shockingly, 67 percent of small farms lose money every year.

These numbers tell us a great deal about the realistic profitability and difficulties of farming, but don't tell us anything about the phenomenon of *microfarms*. Most people who purchase from a CSA or farmers' market are buying from a farm that is far smaller than 200 acres. Those numbers don't accurately represent the local farm. Microfarms usually range in production size from ¼ acre to 20 acres, and unlike *hobby farms* of the same size, they are actually trying to run a business. Seventy-two percent of farms have under 200 acres, up from 60 percent in 1997, and 10 percent of farms are under 10 acres.

The small farm that you might imagine run by a family on a few lush acres and grows a variety of vegetables has become more common in the last ten years. Unfortunately, very, very few of them have made a profit. Most of them are supported by outside employment, with the farmer only farming part time, or with a spouse willing to put income into a project that loses money every year. Tiny farms tend to be more profitable per square foot than the 200-acre farms, but for many it's a way of supplementing the family food budget or contributing to the mortgage payment. They are fragile in the sense that the land value itself is what keeps it afloat. If the family ever needs cash, they will sell it.

So why aren't there more new farms, and why don't farms do better financially? When choosing a career, young people tend to pick jobs with the best outlook. Farming has a pretty terrible outlook by these statistics, so there's not much incentive to enter the field. The majority of young people today don't support industrial agriculture, and there's not much opportunity yet for university-level sustainable agriculture education. This means that college-age students must find apprenticeships, of which there are a limited number, and work in harsh conditions doing hard labor, often for free. Once the student finally feels knowledgeable and decides to start his own farm, he must then acquire hundreds of thousands of dollars in land and equipment. So the student hopes to find some farm loan or grant that will get him started, or even an aging farmer that would kindly let him lease, but these opportunities are rare. As time goes on, the energy and enthusiasm that inspired him in the first place slowly drains away and that new farm never materializes.

So why don't farms make money in general? The USDA statistics are heavily influenced by corn, soybeans, and beef—the three biggest agricultural products in the United States. There are so many farms producing these three things that the bottom of the market for them has all but dropped out. Corn, beef, and soybean prices are too low for the farmer to make a living. The other kind of farm, the small *market* or *truck farm*, is becoming more popular and has a relatively new business model that is still being tweaked for the North American market. This kind of farm is small in size and sells its products from the back of a truck or at the farmers' market. Some farmers are successful, because they manage crop succession well and take care of the soil, and they have a reliable and low-cost distribution method. Many farms are not so great at these things, because they don't treat their farm as a business. You can understand everything about growing food and still fail as a farm if you don't understand business. Many farms fail on the idea that if they grow something, the buyer will magically appear, but the very existence of marketing boards proves that this is not true.

On top of the difficult realities of farming itself, there is growing opposition to the small farm from the government. We talk about factory farming and the government's leniency to the horrible atrocities they are often guilty of, and yet the small farmer is treated much differently. While the factory farm can pay a fine and continue on its merry way, the small farm is often harassed and investigated for years due to imagined offenses that harm no one. In December 2011, Linda "Montana" Jones of Hastings, Ontario, learned that forty-four of her sheep were scheduled to be culled by the Canadian Food Inspection Agency. Culling is the practice of killing animals that don't fit certain breed criteria or who are sick to improve the flock or breed. Wholearth Farmstudio is a conservation farm specializing in preserving rare farm animal breeds that are threatened with extinction. Jones raised Shropshire sheep, a breed that had been brought to North America from England in the late 1800s and at one time was the most popular kind of sheep on this continent, with more than 500,000 registered. With Jones's sheep there were less than 150 ewes and a handful of rams. Why save an old breed of sheep? Unlike breeds that were developed today for factory farming, heritage sheep serve a dual purpose. They are better all-around producers, providing lots of meat, milk, wool, and lambs. Breeds that can do only one thing are genetically limited and usually problematic.

Jones's sheep were targeted for culling because a sheep she had sold to another farm *three years earlier* became infected with scrapie, a neurological disease that only affects sheep and goats. This disease doesn't hurt people at all, and you can still eat the meat from an animal that has it. But it does hurt flocks, and commercial sheep breeders can be devastated by it. The CFIA decided to eradicate all scrapie by killing all the sheep that had it. The only problem is that numerous tests had shown that sheep still actually owned by Jones did not have scrapie, ever.

If Jones defied the culling order, she faced a $250,000 fine and two years in prison. The culling was planned for April 2, 2012, and the CFIA was simply going to show up and take the sheep. However, their plans were dashed when a third party intervened. In the middle of the night, the quarantined sheep scheduled for slaughter were stolen, and a note was left on the door: WE HAVE TAKEN THE ANIMALS INTO PROTECTIVE CUSTODY UNTIL AN ALTERNATIVE TO KILLING HAS BEEN FOUND, OR CONCLUSIVE INDEPENDENT PROOF OR CLEAR EVIDENCE OF DISEASE HAS BEEN PROVEN. THIS HAS BEEN DONE WITHOUT THE KNOWLEDGE OR PARTICIPATION OF THE OWNER. The note was signed: Farmers Peace Corp.

Without any sheep to cull, the CFIA took a sheep that had died of natural causes to perform tests on. They claimed that an autopsy showed that the sheep had died of scrapie, but Jones believes this to be a lie, especially as an independent party did not perform the autopsy. Heartbroken and desperate, Jones made a public plea: "I just want whoever has my flock to bring it back to me and then everybody leave me alone."

No one seemed to know who the Farmers Peace Corp was. In the meantime, the CFIA seized and killed nine of Jones's pregnant ewes to verify their health status. They announced cheerfully that all the sheep tested negative for scrapie. At the same time, Jones has been trying to clear her name. "I've again requested DNA and obex tissue samples from CFIA, so a third party lab can re-test to determine if there was an 'error' in their alleged positive, as all other findings still indicate there is no scrapie in my flock . . . or what's left of them."

With these kinds of financial and regulatory challenges, it's no wonder that small farms are disappearing.

The Useful Bus

Our bus, although a beautiful motor home, was still an aging vehicle that had once taken skiers to Heavenly Ski Resort over and over again. We named her The Albatross, and while she was uncomfortable to drive around in, there was no point in having a bus that stood still. We decided to drive across North America over the summer to tour organic farms. I would interview the farmers and John would take photos, and we could write a book about how to be a successful farmer.

I began contacting hundreds of farms in every region of America, asking them if they would agree to be interviewed and photographed. I had a very strict set of criteria that was designed to ensure that the farms included in the book were truly successful and could be good examples to young farmers just starting out. The response was underwhelming. Of hundreds and hundreds of emails sent out, only twenty-one farmers responded. These twenty-one farms were amazing and beautiful, but I had hoped to have a larger pool of farms to choose from.

We had a mechanic look over the bus and he gave us his stamp of approval, and then we decided to have it commercially inspected before we took such a long trip, just in case there was a little safety issue we had missed. We had about $10,000 saved up for fuel and emergencies, and we were ready to go.

The inspection happened a few days before we were all set to leave on our cross-country trip. We left the bus with the mechanic and spent the day walking at the beach. At the end of the day, we got a call that we would not be able to retrieve our house for a few more days. The brakes were completely shot, and we would need new ones. In fact, we couldn't even take the bus with us anywhere because it was too hazardous. All our belongings were locked in the bus which was at the mechanics, so we borrowed at tent and camped in a friend's backyard, miserably waiting for the prognosis. Unfortunately, the bill was heart-wrenching and took almost our entire budget just before our scheduled send-off.

As devastating as this news was, it allowed me the opportunity to spend the next nine months doing more research on organic farming and some detective work on the farms I wanted to include in my book. In many ways, it was the best thing that could have happened to us. Was I writing a happy picture book, or did I really want to know what was going on?

Taking a Stand

"If the world were merely seductive, that would be easy. If it were merely challenging, that would be no problem. But I arise in the morning torn between a desire to improve the world and a desire to enjoy the world. This makes it hard to plan the day."

—E. B. White

What does it mean to take a stand? This is where knowledge must be turned into action, but what action can we take in a world where everyone lives in a food desert, all our meat comes from factories, and corporations bully farmers into poverty?

Know Your Priorities

Your first voting power is with your purchases. *Locavores,* a group of local foodies in California that grew into a movement, inspired the list of priorities below, but I've changed it based on the research that helped shape my own priorities. It's not the end of the story, or even the solution to the problems, but it's an important start on the road to *not* contributing to the problems we have been talking about.

1. Buy locally produced food. Most locally produced food is naturally grown without chemicals. Any industrial farm located near you is probably shipping their product elsewhere or to the supermarket, so buy directly from your farmer.

2. Support family farms. There are farms that are corporately owned, especially for meat products. Many grocery stores are jumping on the local food bandwagon, so even though it says local, it's a good idea to know the farmers. Ask where things came from and how they were produced.

3. Patronize local businesses. If you can't find it produced on a family farm, then at least buy it from a locally owned business. There is always a tiny business competing against the big supermarket, and putting your money there helps your whole local economy.

4. Know the *terroir*. If not local, purchase artisan products that are specific to the region they were grown or made. Then at least you are supporting farms that are preserving a tradition and flavor and usually have a higher dedication to quality.

5. Buy organic. Organic is a high priority, but mostly because of lesser impact on the environment and avoidance of GM varieties. This is especially important for certain types of products, particularly corn, cotton, and soybeans. If you are buying a corn product, make sure it is truly organic.

Say, for example, that you need to buy cheese. First, you try to find some at the farmers' market, but either you can't find any or it's too expensive. Now you have a couple of choices. You can run down to the locally owned market and buy some cheese there. They are likely to also carry *terroir* French cheeses. If all else fails, and you find yourself at the local grocery store and have to pick between the regular cheese, *terroir* French cheese, or organic cheese, it's a toss up between the French and organic. At this point it pays to know who you are buying from and understand exactly how both cheeses were produced. It's also possible that the chain grocery store carries a locally produced cheese.

It's Not About Buying Stuff

This section was originally called "Battling the Corporations." It was all about buying local, supporting local farmers, and encouraging big factory farms to transform. This is a theory that supports the idea that local farmers are more sustainable, ethical, and possibly safer. However, I've changed my mind somewhat on what the real solution to this problem is. How do we stop using factory farms when we are almost completely dependent on them, and even those farmers are going out of business? No one group of farmers makes a profit. There are a few industrialized farms producing food on a massive scale that definitely make money, and everyone else is struggling. Farming these days means that farmers either have to accept the fact that they will be dirt poor or have to work two jobs to support themselves. It means that it's not a business for most of the people involved in it.

With this in mind, our purchasing power as consumers is not the only solution to the problem. It's an important step, but it's not going to bring about long-term change. The next steps will take much more involvement by individuals and governments.

Corporations, whether they are genetics companies selling chickens to farmers or meat companies selling chickens to consumers, control most of the food. They dictate how it is grown, and they have created a system that does it in a very efficient and low-cost way, to the detriment of everyone's health. They have received government control to such a degree that small, new farmers are sometimes finding themselves inadvertently doing something against the law if they try to produce food in alternative ways. This isn't something that can quickly be solved by a handful of people buying free-range chicken.

The marketing machines would like us to believe that all our food is coming from beautiful green pastures and rolling hills. This does not match the reality of the festering cesspools and toxic chemicals that contaminate most of our farmland. Not all big farms are evil, and not all small farms are good. This is why it is important to know your farmer. Understand how food is grown, where it comes from, and the potential risks you take when you trust other people with something as vital as the food that keeps you alive.

CHAPTER FOUR

Organic Isn't Always Organic

"With the advent of industrial farming and the green revolution, organic farming was relegated to the status of 'quaint' or 'old-fashioned' . . . something practiced by hippies on communes, certainly not by serious farmers."

—David Suzuki

The Definition of *Organic*

"All progress is based upon a universal innate desire on the part of every organism to live beyond its income."

—Samuel Butler

There was a moment, albeit a very brief one, when the term *organic* referred to a method of growing and manufacturing food that required sustainability and the complete absence of chemicals. Early in 1941, English botanist Sir Albert Howard wrote *An Agricultural Testament*, describing alternative organic methods for building soil fertility and health. This was in direct conflict with the science of respected German chemist Justus von Liebig, who had set the standard a hundred years earlier and is considered the father of the modern fertilizer industry. He promoted the idea that plants need only three major components: nitrogen, phosphorous, and potassium (symbolized by their chemical letters NPK), give or take some trace minerals.

Among his many accomplishments were the invention of nitrogen-based fertilizer and Oxo beef bullion.

Von Liebig's method dictated that humus was unimportant, and what plants really needed was intense applications of NPK. Howard, on the other hand, created the Law of Return, which was almost the complete opposite: Whatever comes from the soil must be returned to it. It was an ideology that flew in the face of the Industrial Revolution because it seemed to turn against science and progress. Because of this, Howard saw little credit for his ideas, and his book went out of print; he remained obscure for the rest of his life. The seeds were sown, however. A young man named Jerome (J. I.) Rodale read Howard's *The Soil and Health* and it inspired him so much that it became his life's work. He became a fevered activist, promoting organic growing in his magazine and eventually meeting Howard and inviting him to write some articles. Rodale became the marketing machine for change in the 1930s.

These two men defined *organic* as we know it today. Conventional methods of fertilizing soil today are exactly the same as those invented during the 1840s: adding caustic and potent NPK in its pure forms, thereby killing the soil in the process. The living matter that makes up healthy loam quickly dies under repeated application. Organic growing depends only on the natural waste that comes from the earth to feed plants: the roots and stems left over from harvest, manure from animals, vegetable matter that begins to rot—all the components of a compost pile. Rather than growing bigger plants faster, organic is content with building a higher yield over time through better soil.

For the first few years of his magazine, Rodale targeted farmers, trying to educate them on organic farming. Many hours and wasted dollars later, he realized that most farmers at that time truly didn't care, and he abandoned that effort. Instead he turned to the home gardener and the consumer, who began to really drive the movement forward. It wasn't until the early 1950s, however, when a congressman became sick after exposure to DDT that the term *organic* began to take off as a household word. Congressman James Delaney launched the first government investigation into chemicals used to produce food, and the few organic farmers that did exist at the time whole-heartedly supported this sudden interest politics was taking. Delaney invited J. I. Rodale to speak to Congress, who unfortunately saw him as a romantic without any scientific basis. Rodale in turn felt that the government and the USDA were ignorant and was disgusted with their lack of interest in researching the matter. He was attacked by public relations campaigns on all sides, including Monsanto, who published a propaganda pamphlet with pictures showing naturally grown fields of corn yielding far less than the "modern" land grown with chemicals.

In North America, the organic movement very quickly became political. It was defined by the mistaken idea that people must rebel against the Industrial Revolution, which had so recently granted them so many comforts and luxuries through science. It was seen as a step backwards. There was never a moment when the term *organic* simply meant natural soil health, because government, business, and farmers have been tearing away at it for decades.

Today *organic* can mean any number of things as defined by the USDA organic standards, which were eventually created. However, in it is pure form, true organic means caring for the soil, not the plants. Organic growers feed the soil what came from the soil, and conventional growers feed plants lab-created minerals.

This is an extremely important distinction. In the argument of GMO versus non-GMO and pesticides versus no-pesticides, how do you create proof that this low-tech, humble organic method is the correct one? Proponents of conventional farming and GMOs argue that without these scientific advancements, our ever-increasing population will be at risk of starvation and millions of people will die. They say that organic farms cannot possibly grow enough to meet the demand, which is partly true. There aren't enough organic farms to feed the world. But when we argue about the organic system itself, does it yield as much as conventional agriculture? Clever marketers make arguments about what organic is to discredit it. They define organic as a method that is supposed to be more nutritious and then work to prove that it's not. They define it as pesticide-free and then work to prove that organic farmers are still using chemicals to cast doubt on organic integrity. They define organic as an idyllic farmscape and then work to cast organic farmers as selfish and idealistic. It's a clever game, and it works in the political arena. Of course, the people behind this marketing machine are the same companies that have been there all along selling the chemicals. In this propaganda battle the only defense is a return to the true definition of *organic*: building soil health by returning to the soil what the soil produces.

Where Organic Food Comes From

"A corporation, essentially, is a pile of money to which a number of persons have sold their moral allegiance."

—Wendell Berry

Whole Foods, despite its hip and healthy image, gets a lot of flack. It often finds itself in the center of any organic controversy only because it has stuck its neck out to distribute organic food on a large scale. Whole Foods is dedicated to local food, as evidenced by the beautiful signs all over their store, but the highly touted statistic is that the maximum amount of locally grown produce in a Whole Foods store at any one time is 30 percent. This is in the summer when things are in season. In the winter it may be nothing.

This isn't Whole Food's fault, but the chain gets criticized for it because of its high-gloss marketing. Thirty percent is actually quite high considering how little food is grown in *temperate* regions. Most organic produce grown in the United States comes from California. The rest of it comes from Central and South America. And while we still think of organic farmers as the little guy, that's just not true anymore. Let's take a look at some other organic brands. Many of them are owned by the major food manufacturers:

- Seeds of Change is owned by Mars (makers of M&Ms and many other candies).
- Cascadian Farm is owned by General Mills.
- Boca Foods is owned by Kraft.
- Spectrum Organics is owned by Heinz.
- Honest Tea is owned by Coca Cola.
- Naked Juice is owned by Pepsi.
- Morningstar Farm is owned by Kellogg.
- Nature's Farm is owned by Tyson.

The reality is that almost all organic brands found in the grocery store are owned by a major food company that you are trying to avoid. Even brands that started out independently get purchased and are no longer the little organic companies that you imagine:

- Annie's Homegrown was purchased in 2002 by Solera Capital.
- Stonyfield Farm was purchased in 2001 by Danone.
- Vermont Bread Company was purchased in 2005 by Charter House Group Inc.
- Santa Cruz Organic was purchased in 1989 by Smucker.

It's safe to say that almost all food that arrives in a package with an organic label is owned corporately and came from far away, and while it may be nice to think that we are not supporting chemical companies, buying organic does absolutely nothing for farmers. From 1998 to 2006, direct organic sales, or sales from the farmer direct to the consumer, grew 2 percent, up from almost 1 percent. In the same period of time, organic food that was sold in stores grew at least 12 percent, up from 5 percent, and brings in around a billion dollars per year. It is clear that distributors, not farmers, are eating this organic pie.

Okay, that's not entirely true. The other 70 percent of Whole Food's organic produce does come from farms, but not as you imagine them to be. Take, for example, Earthbound Farms. Anyone in North America buying baby greens has usually seen Earthbound Farms products, and in fact you probably have some in your fridge right now. Started in 1984 on 2.5 acres in California, Earthbound now covers an unbelievable 30,000 acres. This land is located in California, Arizona, Mexico, Washington, Nevada, Argentina, Peru, New Zealand, Brazil, and the Dominican Republic. Baby greens and fruit arrive on grocery store shelves all year-round, through the magic of growing near the equator. It is possible to grow greens year-round in most places, but the yields grown in the perfect light and temperature conditions of the southern United States and northern Mexico are so much greater that it doesn't make sense for a large company to try to grow locally.

Earthbound Farms is high tech, efficient, and the epitome of everything that is right and wrong with organic agriculture. People demand certain vegetables all year-round. They want greens in December in New York and they want them cheap. They also want to ease their conscience and their health anxiety. Earthbound Farms fulfills those desires by supplying what people want: chemical-free greens and fruit in midwinter anywhere in the world. This is clearly better than some other forms of agriculture.

However, we can't call it sustainable. These greens are grown in the desert on a massive scale. Lettuce and spinach need a great deal of water to grow. Unlike some plants that grow well with very little water, greens are water hogs and need plenty of it all the time. In the desert this doesn't come from rainfall. Eighty percent of America's water is used by agriculture, and in the desert most of that water is fed from groundwater sourced from the Colorado River. Approximately 50,000 acres of Arizona land is dedicated to growing lettuce alone, and each acre requires a minimum of 40 inches of water to produce a head of lettuce. Forty inches may not sound like much, but think about it in gallons. It takes 28,000 gallons of water to irrigate one acre with *one inch* of water. 50,000 acres × 40 inches is equal to *56 billion* gallons of water.

About 38 million people rely on the Colorado River to live. It provides fresh water, fuels agriculture, and generates electricity. It feeds Lake Mead, the reservoir behind Hoover Dam and a popular oasis that was at one time full of fish. Today it is a fraction of the size and rapidly decreasing. Marinas have been relocated or abandoned and boat launches hang out over empty space. The Colorado River is fed by snowfall high up in the Rocky Mountains, which makes its way downhill into the canyon below. Snowfall has been decreasing since 2000 and has not recovered, and yet the demand on the river has only increased. Much of it is due to farms like Earthbound, which grow regardless of the environment.

This is how most organic food is produced. While it may be better than conventional farming, it is not a sustainable long-term solution.

USDA Organic Standards

"I am sure that the techniques of organic farming cannot be imprisoned in a rigid set of rules. They depend essentially on the attitude of the farmer. Without a positive and ecological approach, it is not possible to farm organically."

—Lady Eve Balfour, organic activist and author

In 1997, the US Department of Agriculture set down a proposal for an all-encompassing organic standard. It was cumbersome and vague, and for the first time in American history, an industry stepped in to actively push for greater restrictions on itself. An unprecedented 275,000 comments on the proposal helped to shape the USDA organic certification, which finally passed in 2000. However, despite years of work by activists, this standard is still not something to admire. The USDA has made it clear that they do not want the organic program to conflict with reliance on conventional agriculture, as Dan Glickman, Secretary of the USDA at the time, said, "The organic classification is not a judgment about the quality or safety of any product. . . . Just because something is labeled as organic does not mean it is superior, safer or more healthy than conventional food."

Only four years after its creation, industry and government officials began trying to change the standards. In 2004 the USDA decided that organic fertilizers could contain "unknown" materials, that sick organic dairy cows could be fed antibiotics, and that nonagricultural products could call themselves organic arbitrarily. Consumers and farmers were in an uproar, knowing that these kinds of loopholes are precisely the kind of thing that the rest of the industry wants to have just so they can capitalize on the organic label. The USDA retracted the changes, but then a month later changed its mind on one of them: Nonagricultural products can still call themselves organic because they are no longer regulated. This includes body care products, dog food, fish, clothing, and more. Chances are that the shampoo and T-shirt you bought thinking they were organic probably aren't.

Only a couple of years later there were more changes. Previously, synthetic additives of any type were banned from organic baby formula, but today more than 90 percent of organic formula contains the synthetic fatty acids DHA or ARA. This is often an advertising feature on the label as a benefit for healthy baby development because it is true that the human body needs fatty acids. The problem is that baby formula manufacturers are using substances that are not related to the natural fatty acids a baby would get from mother's milk. They are extracted from algae and fungus using hexane, a strong neurotoxin. While the manufacturers assure us that no hexane residue exists in the final product, it is not organic in the same sense that organic tomatoes are.

This is the equivalent of washing a conventionally grown tomato very, very well so that no pesticide residue remains, and calling it organic.

That was in 2006. A few years later, as government administration changed, so did the USDA guidelines. The new USDA administration discovered that the baby formula and organic milk rules were changed under the table, after a few casual email exchanges between USDA program manager Barbara Robinson and baby formula industry lawyer William Friedman. This serious breach of the system went under review in 2010, and it was announced that synthetic additives would again be banned. At the time of this writing, they haven't actually been banned, but the USDA assures that they will be.

Baby formula is just the tip of the iceberg. Let's take a look at just a few of the many ways that the USDA organic standards are lacking. Originally, to be able to achieve certification, a product could have no more than 5 percent approved nonorganic substances. This list of approved substances was supposed to serve as a way of transitioning the industry to stricter organic standards so that the list would eventually disappear. It started with 75 substances and is now at 245. Some of these are necessary and benign, such as using dish soap to counteract certain insect infestations, and some are not so nice. Xanthan gum, for example, is an artificial thickener. It is created by fermenting sugars with a certain bacteria, then drying and grinding it into a powder. It is usually in your toothpaste and probably in your laxatives. It was tested on animals in the 1960s and approved for food use, but the effects on pregnant women and children are unknown. It can lower blood sugar levels, and it swells in the intestine, which is why it makes such a good laxative. It is now also in your organic food.

The reason there are more items on the list than there were before is because of lobbying by the Organic Trade Association. Rather than a group of farmers out to improve organic standards, the OTA is made of corporate interests such as Kraft and Dole who want to relax the standards so they can keep making the same old stuff under new and more lucrative labels. It is much easier and cheaper to change the rules than to play the game differently.

So instead of banning substances, the USDA created new kinds of labeling:

100% Organic – This is the pure form. The product must be made with all organic ingredients.

Organic – This is actually 95 percent organic. The other 5 percent can include things like xanthan gum, but it draws the line at sewage, pesticides, or irradiation (killing harmful organisms with radiation).

Made with Organic Ingredients – This is 70 percent organic. These products can't carry the USDA seal, but they can list up to three things that are organic. They can also use sewage sludge disguised as fertilizer, irradiation, and pesticides.

New wording opened a flood of products into the organic market. You might think that there has been improvement because you see so many more organic products on the shelf, but the reality is that the standards changed and allowed more in.

Clever combinations of words are also permitted. For example, let's suppose I decided to sell flaxseed crackers. If I label them as "Organic Flaxseed Crackers," then the entire cracker is 95 percent organic. If I label them as "Flaxseed Organic Crackers," then the flax seed is not organic but the rest of the cracker is 95 percent organic. It allows me to actually have more than 5 percent nonorganic substances in my cracker, but still profit from the labeling.

The same loopholes can be found in every aspect of the organic standard. For example, according to the strictest definition of organic farming, cows eat grass and nothing else. Feeding them grain is considered a method of artificial fattening. However, the USDA organic standard has created wording that gets around this problem:

100% Grass Fed – The cattle are raised on pasture from birth until death.

Grass Fed/Finished on pasture with supplemental grain – The cattle start on grass, but grain is brought in to speed things along.

Grass Fed/Grain Finished – The cattle start on pasture but are moved to a regular feedlot, packed together, and stuffed with grain for 90 to 160 days before slaughter. Considering these cattle only live fourteen months, this makes up almost half of their short lives.

The idea that real organic farmers somehow lobbied for this kind of allowable treatment of cattle is laughable. The only reason the USDA would include beef that had experienced the horrors of a feedlot is because of corporate interests who simply want to label conventional beef organic without having to make any changes.

In 2002, Maine farmer Arthur Harvey filed a civil lawsuit against USDA Secretary Ann Veneman challenging the National Organic Program. He was attempting to prove that the NOP was inconsistent with the Organic Foods Production Act. The OFPA was part of the 1990 Farm Bill, and its purpose was to launch the organic program, define *organic* for labeling purposes, and dictate how the government should interpret it. In his case he asked the court to reverse the decision that allowed synthetic substances to be added to organic foods. He had a list of specific substances that should have never been allowed. For two years he represented himself without a lawyer, while the judge and Veneman's lawyer quibbled about which items on the list he actually had a case on. Finally the judge found in favor of Veneman (and the USDA) on all counts except for one. Arthur Harvey then acquired a lawyer and filed an appeal along with many other interested parties, including the Organic Consumers Association, Sierra Club, Greenpeace, The Center for Food Safety, and others. After a yearlong legal battle, the judge sided with Harvey on three of seven issues. The key win was that the allowance of synthetic substances in processed foods did indeed go against the spirit of the OFPA.

There was a great deal of discussion and anxiety in 2005 when this happened. There was speculation that the USDA would take the whole organic act and try to rewrite it, or that the whole synthetic list would have to be reviewed on an item-by-item basis, taking years and precious dollars. Unfortunately, Congress immediately amended the OFPA with wording that specifically overruled Harvey's win. The Organic Foods Production Act now said that synthetic substances can be added to organic foods, expanded how they are added to the list of allowable substances, and also threw in a new allowance: Nonorganic feed could now be fed to organic dairy cows in certain situations.

Harvey retaliated with an appeal, but the court found in favor of the USDA very quickly. It is unlikely that any future lawsuit would be able to bring about change because of this legal precedent.

The National List is a serious thing. It is the list of allowable substances that makes or breaks the organic standard. Who is in charge of this list?

The members of the National Organic Standards Board are solely responsible for recommendations to remove and add materials to the list. Everything has to go through this board of fifteen people. It must have at least four farmers/producers, three environmentalists, three consumer advocates, one retailer, one scientist, and one USDA certifying agent. In 2005, when Arthur Harvey's case was coming to a conclusion, there were people on the board who probably had a vested interest in its integrity, or at least an unbiased opinion, such as

- Rigoberto Delgado, owner of Delgado Farms, a certified organic farm in Texas
- Goldie Caughlan, founder of a cooking school for PCC Natural Markets food co-op in Seattle
- Dennis Holbrook, owner of South Texas Organics, an organic citrus farm
- Bea E. James, an educator for natural food co-ops

- Hubert J. Karreman, a veterinarian specializing in holistic organic cow care
- Rosalie L. Koenig, owner of Rosie's Organic Farm
- Dr. Michael P. Lacy, a scientist and professor interested in poultry science
- Jeff Moyer, farm director at Rodale Institute
- Dr. Nancy M. Ostiguy, scientist and professor specializing in pesticides and impact on insects
- James Riddle, organic farmer and certification inspector
- George Siemon, organic farmer and organic farm coop consultant

There were also a few that probably didn't have the same interests, such as

- **Andrea Caroe** was the executive director of an independent certifying body called Protected Harvest. Protected Harvest is an organization that tries to help conventional farmers stay below a certain toxicity level. Today she owns her own green certification company called EarthClaims that helps companies and farms get many different kinds of certifications. She may be knowledgeable about certification, but her training and education had nothing to do with environmental science, which was unfortunately her position on the board.
- **David Carter** is the principal of Crystal Springs Consulting Group. His work involves helping farmers, specifically beef producers, find new marketing channels. His interest in organic certification is in trying to find new ways to sell beef, but he was on the board as a representative of Consumer/Public Interest. Whose interest was he representing, consumers or beef producers?
- **Kevin O'Rell** is the president of research and development and organic certification at Horizon Organic. Horizon is the largest organic dairy company in the United States and is owned by Dean Foods, a major food processor. It was also in the center of controversy in 2006, when the Organic Consumers Association and Cornucopia

Institute accused the company of violating organic standards. However, O'Rell was on the board as a producer. Was he a farmer or another executive looking out for corporate interests?

- **Gerald Davis** was an agronomist and pest control advisor at Grimmway Farms, the largest grower and distributor of carrots in the world. His position on the board as "organic producer" was interesting considering that his job at Grimmway has nothing to do with its organic division specifically. Grimmway uses "integrated pest control" on most of its crops, which in many cases means the use of pesticides according to insect lifecycles rather than according to a set calendar.

- **Daniel Giacomini,** an animal nutritionist, owns Pacific Nutrition-Consulting, a firm specializing in consulting for the organic industry. He was on the board as another Consumer/Public Interest representative, but just like David Carter, he actually represents producers, not consumers or public interest. His job is to help farmers transition to organic and find "strategies for redesigning existing products to meet organic regulations at the least cost to the company."

- **Julie Weisman** was the Vice President of Organic Product Development for Elan Chemical Company, a business specializing in synthetic and natural flavors and scents for food and perfume. She was listed on the board as "handler," but as the only company with a representative on the board who actually produces synthetics, no one else had a greater interest in controlling the synthetics list than she did.

Six of fifteen board members (40 percent) at that time had a conflict of interest in their decision making as members of the board. Hopefully we can give the others the benefit of the doubt, but the situation is no different today. Perhaps there is a place for the opposite point of view—synthetic producers across the table from organic farmers, and corporate dairy conglomerates against small farms. However, these individuals have been jammed into positions that aren't even remotely close to their actual job descriptions, and it's quite a stretch of the imagination to see how they fit. Executives aren't producers, certification experts aren't environmentalists, and agricultural consultants have no business representing public interest.

Grassroots Organic Alternatives

The word *organic* is now proprietary. By law, in the United States and Canada, you can only use that word to describe food and products if you have paid for the government-regulated label. This is why independent bodies have to use words like *natural, sustainable*, and *nonpolluting* instead.

Certified Naturally Grown: This program is for small producers, with lower fees and a Participatory Guarantee System. Farmers are annually inspected by their peers, as the CNG website describes: "While the PGS concept is still new to many in the United States, PGS programs have been in place for decades. They are typically a better fit for small-scale direct-market farmers, and they foster local farmer networks to strengthen the farming community through mutual support and educational opportunities." Although the standards aren't really stricter than the USDA standard, this program allows farmers who can't afford the steep cost of organic certification to prove that they are growing with organic practices. CNG is the largest alternative in North America and to date more than 800 farms carry the label.

Montana Sustainable Grower's Union: The Homegrown label was the first of its kind in North America. Montana growers were the first to replace the national organic standard with a strictly local organic label. It also uses a peer review system to ensure farmers are really doing what they say they are, and it is a trusted brand in Montana. Unlike CNG, the Homegrown label has higher standards in many ways.

Kootenay Local Agricultural Society: The Kootenay Mountain Grown label mirrors the Montana label, but it is even more localized to foods grown within the Kootenay region of British Columbia. It also uses the peer review system and also has some higher standards than the USDA label.

This is the extent of the independent certifying bodies in North America. All the others, including Oregon Tilth and other state-specific programs, are actually just certification agents of the USDA organic program. The International Federation of Organic Agricultural Movements (IFOAM) oversees the alternative programs. PGS certifying groups are defined as: "locally focused quality assurance systems. They certify producers based on active participation of stakeholders and are built on a foundation of trust, social networks and knowledge exchange."

Dignity: You Are What You Eat

"In 2010, nearly 50 million American households were listed as food insecure. As you can imagine, when you're worried about having enough money to buy food for your family, whether or not the food you do manage to buy is making you fat is probably not a top concern. Bad food is better than no food."

—Morgan Clendaniel of Co.EXIST

There are many, many books available today about obesity in America, and this isn't one of them. Chances are that at some point you have struggled with your weight or had health issues that were directly linked to your diet, and you might not even have been aware of it. That's just the reality of the situation. The vast majority of us can't afford or even get access to truly fresh vegetables and fruit, which should be making up the bulk of our diets. Meanwhile, the government publishes food guides that are little better than propaganda for marketing boards. These USDA food guides might make us feel better mentally but they are definitely not good for us physically.

The food groups were invented in the early 1900s by the USDA and originally had eight groups. Those first food groups included milk products, oranges/tomatoes/grapefruit, green and yellow vegetables, eggs, meat, breads, butter, and other fruits and vegetables. You were supposed to eat a total of four servings of fruit and vegetables per day. In the 1940s the groups were down to seven: milk, veggies, fruits, eggs, meat and cheese, cereal and bread, and butter. Fruits and vegetables per day were still at four servings. We were supposed to drink two glasses of milk, eat one serving of meat or cheese, two servings of cereal and bread, and two tablespoons of butter every day.

In the 1950s the groups were down to four: milk, meat, fruit and vegetables, and bread. We were still at four servings of fruit and vegetables, and two glasses of milk, meat and eggs were combined into two servings, but bread was increased to four servings. It is easy to see that up until this time, the USDA promoted a diet that had double the fruits and vegetables that it did meat.

In the 1990s the USDA switched to a food pyramid. This highly promoted pyramid had a big base of bread, requiring 6–11 servings, with fruit and vegetables in the middle at 5–9 servings, and meat and dairy on top with 4–6 servings. This was an extreme change, and meat and dairy had taken on almost the same importance as vegetables and fruit. Then in 2005 this was replaced by another pyramid that showed ratios rather than servings for each group. This pyramid was even more vague, and meat and dairy were given just as large a ratio as vegetables and fruit.

In 2012 this changed again, removing the pyramid altogether and replacing it with a pie chart that looks like a plate. Fruits and vegetables make up half the plate, with grain and protein making up the other half, and a glass of dairy on the side. The dairy ratio is difficult to compare since it is separate from the rest. This plate is an improvement on the previous iteration, because at least fruit and vegetables appear to have a majority share. However, the USDA websites says that "fruits may be fresh, canned, frozen, or dried, and may be whole, cut-up, or pureed." There is no mention of the greater value of fresh foods over canned ones, and one could construe that a can of peaches in a sugary syrup is just as good as a fresh peach. It also has a guide to portions based on age. A woman my age needs 2 cups of fruit and 2.5 cups of vegetables per day, but the protein guideline somehow doesn't match what the pie is telling me. It says I need 5.5 ounces per day, which they say is the equivalent of one medium steak, two lean hamburgers, or three cups of lentils.

Besides the obvious disparity between steak and lentils, I don't know about you, but if I ate two hamburgers every day I would become increasingly overweight and would no longer have the energy and health I now enjoy. Several studies directly contradict these recommendations, such as one done in 2009, published by the Archives of Internal Medicine, and funded by the National Cancer Institute. This study observed participants over a ten-year span and found that 11 percent of male deaths and 16 percent of female deaths might have been prevented if they had eaten less red meat. The study associated higher cancer and cardiovascular mortality rates with red meat, and those two things happen to be the leading causes of death in the United States. The results of this study confirm the findings of a study done in 2008 by World Cancer Research Fund International, which also found a link between red meat, cancer, and heart health.

However, the marketing boards were quite offended by these studies. The Pork Board's dietician at the time, Ceci Snyder, said that the study by the NCI "attempts to indict all red meat consumption by looking at extremes in meat consumption, as opposed to what most Americans eat" (Ruiz). The USDA says that the average American is eating 3.7 ounces of meat and poultry a day, but this conflicts with the National Health and Nutrition Examination Survey conducted by the Center for Disease Control. This prestigious and accurate survey interviewed 18,000 people and found that the average person eats 7 ounces of meat and poultry per day, with red meat making up 58 percent of that and 22 percent of it processed. This means that the average American is eating 4 ounces of red meat, plus 3 ounces of chicken every day, and 1.5 ounces of it is processed (Daniel). These aren't the "extremes in meat consumption"—these are the averages.

In 2001 the Physicians Committee for Responsible Medicine (a non-profit organization with 9,000 members) filed a lawsuit against the USDA to bring "national attention to the heavy influence of the meat, dairy, and egg industries in the creation of federal food policies." They won, surprisingly, and the US District Court ruled that the USDA violated federal law by withholding documents revealing bias among the dietary advisory panel. As it turns out, the council had included people representing the National Dairy Council, the National Cattlemen's Beef Association, the American Egg Board, and the National Dairy Promotion and Research Program Board. In 2011, PCFM filed another lawsuit that called for an end to ambiguous and deceptive language in the food guidelines. "For example," they said, "the Dietary Guidelines specify foods to eat more frequently (e.g., fruits and vegetables), but avoid identifying foods that people need to eat less often (e.g., meat and cheese), instead, the Dietary Guidelines use biochemical terms unfamiliar to the general public, calling for limiting 'cholesterol,' 'saturated fats,' and 'solid fats' without clearly explaining that meat, dairy products, and eggs are the only sources of cholesterol in the diet, dairy products are the number-one source of saturated fat, and meat and dairy products deliver the majority of solid fats in the American diet" (Carman). In conjunction, they released their own food guide, which didn't have any meat in it at all. As of today there doesn't seem to be any conclusion to this legal battle.

The Center for Consumer Freedom spends a great deal of time and effort trying to discredit the PCRM, even running its own website called Physician Scam that is designed solely to cast doubt on PCRM's health message. This organization describes itself as "a nonprofit coalition of restaurants, food companies, and consumers working together to promote personal responsibility and protect consumer choices." They fail to mention the alcohol and tobacco companies also involved. CCF actively works to reverse smoking bans and raise legal blood-alcohol levels, and criticizes anyone who warns against overfishing, pesticides, processed and fatty foods, and soda. It was founded by Richard Berman, professional lobbyist and owner of a Washington, D.C., public affairs firm. From their own website the accusations are worded to sound legitimate, but border on the ridiculous: "PCRM has created a separate deceptive charity called The Cancer Project to help push an animal-rights diet on some of the most vulnerable Americans. The Cancer Project, which shares staff, funding, and even an office with PCRM, is devoted to advancing a fringe anti-meat agenda and promoting the false belief that only a strict vegan diet can minimize the risk of cancer." Only a Washington lobbyist could call a healthy vegetarian diet a "fringe anti-meat agenda." The PCRM has to waste its time in defense against a loud and utterly ludicrous organization that does nothing but promote selfish industry profits, while trying to spread actual scientific evidence for healthy diets, and the USDA is content to remain quiet in the midst of it.

We already know that the USDA isn't trustworthy, but this is a clear lack of respect for the American people. We live in a world where the wealthy nations have just as many malnourished people as the poorest ones, but the cause is manipulation by corporate interests. We are not even granted the dignity of a food guide that reflects modern scientific knowledge, because it steps on the toes of a few major companies. This dietary pattern is taught to millions of children in school, and it will affect their food choices as they grow. With the increasing problems that we face, how can we be feeding them information that will only serve to harm them in the future? This is the crux of the food security problem. Whether we will be able to achieve global food security will remain in the hands of companies and governments who willingly manipulate us (and our children)—unless we take back our dignity and our food.

Solving the World's Food Supply Problem

"One farmer says to me, 'You cannot live on vegetable food solely, for it furnishes nothing to make bones with'; and so he religiously devotes a part of his day to supplying his system with the raw material of bones; walking all the while he talks behind his oxen, which, with vegetable-made bones, jerk him and his lumbering plow along in spite of every obstacle."

—Henry David Thoreau

We barely have any arable land, and the farmland we do have is rapidly degrading and disappearing. Corporations and governments have no regard for the future and are poisoning everything and everyone. Our organic standards are manipulated and changed for the sake of greed and profits, and scientists tell us the only way to feed everyone is to impregnate our food with even more chemicals.

It seems a little hopeless, and as our story continues it doesn't get much better. However, it's not quite as bleak as you might think. Just because the word *organic* has been hijacked and our standards are corrupt, doesn't mean that organic growing itself is somehow a lost cause or suspect in some way. Just because the system is broken doesn't mean we can't find a new one.

In 2002, Per Pinstrup-Andersen, professor of Food, Nutrition, and Public Policy at Cornell University, analyzed 200 studies of organic growing along with his colleagues, and found that organic yields are at least 80 percent of conventional yields. This was a major finding, mostly because the USDA had estimated that organic yields are about 25 percent of conventional yields. In the argument over conventional versus organic, detractors almost always jump to yield as the highest failing of organic growing. It is impossible, they say, for organic methods to produce enough food for the world's population, but this is obviously not true. Losing 20 percent of a yield isn't the end of the world. As Pinstrup-Andersen says, the challenge is not just about having enough food, but also "to continue the expansion of food production to meet future demand without negative effects on the environment. The other major food-related challenge is to assure that everyone has access to sufficient food to live a healthy and productive life." Conventional farming may yield slightly more, but fails miserably on the last two requirements.

His chief motivation for completing the study was not only to provide healthy food to millions of wealthy first-world people, but also to billions of hungry people living in poverty. At the time of that study, about 20 percent of the world's population earned less than a dollar a day, and 800 million of those people lived mouthful to mouthful. Most of us in our privileged societies cannot conceive of what it is like to be so food insecure, and yet it is our own food insecurity that is simultaneously making us increasingly obese. Malnutrition kills, whether it makes us fat or skinny. If our conventional farming in North America is so magnificent, then why are we so malnourished that we have the most obese people in the world?

Government regulation is obviously failing us. It is true that regulation is needed to protect consumers, but in almost every agricultural industry, government regulation favors corporate interests and profits over the interests of small organic farmers.

There's obviously not just one solution. Just as the problems are complex, so is the road to change. The first problem is what people are eating. As the Irish potato famine has proven, if we put all our eggs into one basket we are likely to fail. In third world countries sometimes the solution is as simple as choosing a different variety that needs less water. In first world countries we are doing two things very, very wrong. We eat almost only grain, and we eat too much meat. Not only do we eat too much meat, we feed the meat grain, too. Neither the cattle nor we are supposed to eat that much grain. It takes much less land space to grow things like beans and vegetables, both of which can supply every part of human nutrition.

It all comes down to calories. The average person needs 2,000 calories each day to live. According to the government-recommended diet, it takes at least 1.3 acres to produce enough calories for you to live a healthy life. A vegetarian diet, however, only requires about a tenth of an acre, or 4,300 square feet. This is generally the size of the average American suburban yard. In some warm climates we can do even better than that. We don't even have to be fully vegetarian—this can include some fish and chicken and still use far less than 1.3 acres. However, commercial meat production uses up to fifty times the land area of plant crops to produce the same amount of calories, because it is woefully inefficient.

Not everyone is going to become vegetarian. However, the simplest solution is often the best, and reducing the amount of land it takes to feed each person is the first step to a sustainable food system. Without a severe cutback on the amount of wheat, corn, and soybeans we consume, which includes what we eat through our beef addiction, our food system will not change. This means that most of us have to eat way more vegetables than we are comfortable with.

Many people are also unaware that the government has been subsidizing grain production for ethanol. In a misguided attempt at promoting biofuels, more grain is being grown than ever before just to be converted and burned up as fuel, but it's not even as simple as that. With our ever-growing need for oil, this ethanol is filling a massive gap that would otherwise drive fuel prices up even further. Our oil addiction needs to be kept under control, as well. The subsidy ended at the beginning of 2012, but production requirements are still in place according to a law created in 2005. We are hamsters trapped in a hamster wheel, with no end in sight.

Free and open sharing of knowledge is also necessary. Growing techniques will change, and as small farms develop more efficient ways of growing food sustainably, these methods need to be openly shared with others. The principles of "open source" should be fully embraced in agriculture because they are necessary for our survival. We need to eat and the idea of patenting food or the way it is grown should be as alien as owning air. Open source does not mean free; hard work should be rewarded. But it does mean that the knowledge itself is open and transparent for anyone to use and improve on. Open source requires a community of people dedicated to the idea of putting in effort to making something better. In agriculture this is absolutely crucial, especially with the desperate need for young people to enter farming.

We know that organic farms have the capability of producing almost as much as conventional farms; we just don't have enough of them yet. We don't have enough of them yet because not enough people are eating the right things yet. We also don't have quite enough young people getting into farming. None of the problems with organic food have anything to do with the way the food is grown. The strategies and techniques are sound. What we have is a people problem.

The Four (Real) Food Groups

Fruit – Three or more servings each day of a wide variety of fresh fruits, and at least one serving that is high in Vitamin C, like citrus, melons, and strawberries.

Legumes – Two or more servings per day of beans, peas, chickpeas, soymilk, tofu, and lentils. Choose a wide variety of colors.

Grains – Five or more servings per day of bread, pasta, rice, cereal, corn, millet, barley, bulgur, buckwheat, groats, tortillas. Each meal should be built around a whole grain dish.

Vegetables – Four or more servings per day of a wide variety of colors, including dark green leafy vegetables, and dark yellow and orange vegetables.

A serving is about ½ cup to 1 cup. You don't need meat to survive, but it's no big deal to have a little chicken or fish now and then. Not only will this diet make you healthier, it makes our future better.

(*from PCRM Power Plate*)

Eating Seasonally

Eating seasonally is a more challenging goal than even eating more whole foods or less meat. Many people forget that eating local means eating only what is in season, and that's a tough thing to swallow sometimes. No more tomatoes and peppers in the winter? How can anyone stay healthy without fruit in January? My home on Vancouver Island has a warmer growing season than any other place in Canada. We can grow kiwis and peaches, something that doesn't happen anywhere else in the True North. But fruit still doesn't grow here in the winter. You have to live in the south to do that, which means that most people in North America should be canning and freezing the summer harvest.

Up until June the varieties available in the Pacific Northwest will be brassicas like chards, broccoli, and kale, with some other greens and asparagus thrown in. Kale and chard have enough vitamin C and other minerals to keep you healthy until the fruit comes back, but with some canned fruit and stored vegetables like potatoes and carrots from last year, it's not a far stretch to continue eating local throughout the year. Your diet just has to be simpler.

You are statistically likely to be following the Western Pattern Diet, a manner of eating that has you ingesting lots of red meat, high-fat foods, sugary treats, and refined grains (like white bread). Medical experts know that this diet has severe side effects, but fortunately the solutions are simple (just difficult to choose):

- Stop eating out. Restaurants, unless they are specifically catering to the healthy crowd, are going to be serving you too much food, and the wrong kinds. It's probably not local either.
- Eat a plant-based diet. When transitioning to this kind of diet, I am not sure which is worse, switching slowly, or going cold turkey. The cravings for meat and sweets can be overwhelming. Having chicken and fish and homemade sweets now and then can help you be successful.
- Learn your growing season. When can you pick blackberries? When do tomatoes ripen? What kinds of greens can be grown in the winter? It takes practice to focus your meals around whatever is available. It means forgetting your preplanned menu, and if there's lots of zucchini, eating lots of zucchini. This year we had a huge carrot crop, and we ate carrots in salads, in soups, in wraps, in juice, and in cake. It takes a bit of creativity.

- Keep meals simpler with fewer ingredients. Our meals start with rice, pasta, or quinoa. Then we add vegetables, either raw or blended into a sauce (like pesto), or stir-fried. Then we add salad on the side. Sometimes we take the whole thing and put it in a wrap. For dessert it might be a treat or a pineapple. We wouldn't normally eat pineapple because it doesn't grow here, but it makes a good dessert now and then. To take away the monotony, we add in homemade condiments like pickled cucumbers and beans, fermented kimchi and dressing.

The Road Trip that Didn't Happen

During my nine-month opportunity to research more, I created a survey of questions and sent them out to my twenty-one farmers in the hopes that I could glean some information from them before we arrived and maybe weed out any that didn't belong. There were questions about what they grew, why they got into farming, and very pointed questions about profits. A handbook for young people on organic farming would be useless without some discussion about money. I hoped the farmers would answer even a few questions and waited.

I had a manuscript due for *The Ultimate Guide to Permaculture*, and the bus was parked on a friend's property, an organic farm in the making. We helped them stack wood, had delicious potluck dinners, and caught runaway horses.

We celebrated our second anniversary of living in the bus without really going anywhere.

Stopping to write about permaculture in the middle of all this was the one thing that maintained my sanity. It brought me back to why we had a bus in the first place. As I delved deeper into permaculture and did more research about organic farming, it made me wonder if maybe we were on the wrong track. I still hadn't heard back from any farmers with any answers to my deeper questions, and it seemed like a sign that somehow my assumptions were wrong. I had so many questions for them, and they remained unanswered. I heard tirades about government and rants about pesticides and very little practical information that I could use. On my own, I learned what was really going on in the organic industry, and I realized I needed to write a much different book. Not a book that would only serve as propaganda for the organic industry.

When the permaculture book was done, I reached a final conclusion. It's not *organic* that was going to save the world, as I had so glibly assumed. It was *local*.

Organic Can't Do It

"The more we pour the big machines, the fuel, the pesticides, the herbicides, the fertilizer and chemicals into farming, the more we knock out the mechanism that made it all work in the first place."

—David R. Brower

Science Says One Thing . . .

In the last section I barely mentioned organic yield. Per Pinstrup-Andersen's finding that organic growing techniques produce at least 80 percent of the yield of conventional methods is a good study, but doesn't convince naysayers. Fortunately there are many more good studies that back up organic growing.

The Rodale Institute, the same one begun by J. I. Rodale, which still publishes the magazine that started everything in the first place, has been running a Farming System Trial since 1981. To date, it has gathered thirty years of information by growing organic and conventional crops side by side in Pennsylvania silty loam. The crops grown are the same ones that are in the midst of so much conflict and controversy: corn and soybeans. In 2005 the Institute published a report on its findings. Over the previous twenty-two years, the organically grown crops produced just as much as the conventional ones. In fact, the organic methods used 30 percent less energy in the process. A Cornell University professor of ecology and agriculture, David Pimental, analyzed the study and published his own report, stating, "Organic farming approaches for these crops not only use an average of 30 percent less fossil energy but also conserve more water in the soil, induce less erosion, maintain soil quality and conserve more biological resources than conventional farming does." But wait, skeptics ask, doesn't Rodale have a very biased view? Of course they are going to find in favor of organic. What else would they do, close down everything and just admit conventional is better?

The study was performed in cooperation between unbiased institutions including USDA Agricultural Research Service microbiologists and an agricultural economist from the University of Maryland. What was most interesting about their finding is that during the first four years, organic corn produced far less than conventional corn. Then, over time, the organic corn began producing far higher yields, especially during dry periods. When you add it up, producing 30 percent less than conventional yields for four years is nothing compared to yielding 22 percent more for the remaining eighteen years. Weather was gradually eroding the soil in the conventional field, but with cover crops, organic compost, and better crop rotation, the soil in the organic field got better and better and was able to retain moisture. Remember, organic isn't about pesticides, it's about building the soil.

Considering that the whole argument for GMO corn and soybeans is to producer higher yields with less energy, and studies are showing it doesn't really do that, why does the industry ignore these kinds of studies? Oh, wait . . . it's because they aren't in the business of growing *more* food, it's because they are in the business of *owning* all the food.

The Field Says Otherwise

For all our fantastic science, things are quite a bit different in the real world. According to the USDA surveys of crop yields, the yields for most organic crops tend to be far less than conventional yields if you add together all the Certified Organic crops grown across the United States. The trouble is that only 1 percent of farmland is organic. This is far less than other countries that have a much smaller land base, including Switzerland, Italy, and Uruguay. Our organic farms are not a very good cross-section of farmland, and not a big enough pool of examples to compare with. That doesn't really excuse organic farmers from producing good yields, however. Why is it that under laboratory conditions organic farming is a resounding success, but in actual practice things aren't so rosy?

Of course, once again, the answer is complex. There haven't been any studies comparing the myriad growing methods used by organic farmers or surveys asking how long the farmers have been growing organically or how confident the farmers are in their practices. There's just scientific data on how the farmers are doing what they are doing. Are they growing intensively? Have they built up the soil? How much experience do they have?

The other issue is that organic grain farming is much easier than organic vegetable farming, and organic fruit farming is by far the most difficult. Grain farming is a battle over weeds and weather, but other crops are far more susceptible to pests, fungus, and diseases. Can vegetable and fruit farming catch up to organic grain farming in successful yields?

Unfortunately there's no sure answer to that question until we jump in and find out, but when the alternative is GMO, there doesn't seem like much of a choice. If we want a sustainable food system, then growing enough food will have to become the responsibility of a lot more people. Organic growing is profitable with lower yields simply because the price of the produce is higher, but organic farmers don't make any more money than anyone else because the cost of labor is higher. This is because these farms are smaller and less mechanized, and so more things—like weeding, picking, washing, marketing, and selling—are done by the farmer and a few assistants, rather than by big machines, separate processing facilities, marketing boards, and stores. The low price of conventional foods is directly tied to shortcuts in labor that result in an unsustainable system.

This is a difficult dilemma. The argument over organic versus nonorganic is really an argument of having food in the future versus not having food in the future. The world's population is exploding and food is expensive. Where will food come from in the future if we don't have enough farmers and farmland to grow it ourselves? Is growing without chemicals a viable road to a well-fed future?

Unfortunately, North America is terribly backwards in its farming practices. Other countries have made great strides towards increasing their food security and have done so by increasing organic agriculture. Governments that recognize the economic sense (note that this is not the same as *business* sense) of small-scale agriculture have heavily supported this progress. One of the greatest examples is, surprisingly, Russia. During the Communist era, when the Soviet agricultural program was failing and the country was facing starvation, the government formally recognized the traditional small plots of land people had staked claims to, and granted these people the right to grow food and construct dwellings on them. These little country cottages and gardens, or *dachas*, became extraordinarily popular even though no one owned the land and technically they leased it from the government. Russians began growing their own food out of necessity, and as they became wary of the toxic chemicals in the environment, the fact that it was organic was a huge bonus. When the Soviet Union collapsed, all that land returned to private ownership. Today at least half of all Russians living in the city have a second home in the country on their *dacha*.

By 1999, these millions of little family plots were producing incredible amounts of food. Over 75 percent of the vegetables, 85 percent of the fruit, 55 percent of the meat, and 50 percent of the milk consumed by the Russian population was grown on *dachas* that year (Sharaskin). In 2003 this incredible effort was recognized by the Private Garden Plot Act, which granted any citizen a free inheritable plot of land from the government, a little larger than the previous arrangement. Produce grown on them is organic and nontaxable.

This right to land access has spontaneously created a sustainable, organic food system that grows enough food for Russia's population. In a place plagued by economic and political turmoil, the land has provided food security for millions of Russians. Even more importantly, it has done so without chemicals or GMOs in a harsh climate.

Organic methods are feeding populations all over the world. Detractors would have us believe that a system that only works on a small scale over many individually owned plots couldn't possibly be sustainable. They only say this because it can't be globalized and monetized to their benefit.

Organic Growing

"The accomplice to the crime of corruption is frequently our own indifference."

—Bess Myerson

One of the biggest misconceptions about organic food is its nutritional value, and I'm going to start out by saying that there's no proof that organic food has more nutrients than conventional food. There's also no proof that it doesn't. One thing is certain: Organic food is not *less* nutritious. There's just so much conflicting information and none of it is complete.

It is true that local food is the most nutritious by far. But fresh isn't the same as organic, which simply has to do with the soil. To the plants, nutrients are all the same, whether they come from chemicals or dirt. While extra minerals from organic compost might make their way into a fruit, all we can assume is that a strawberry is a strawberry no matter how it was grown.

There are many reasons, other than ourselves, to support organic farming. Here are just a few:

- **The soil.** The plants may not know the difference between organic and conventional farming on a chemical level, but they feel it later when it rains and the soil dries out faster. The soil can be depleted and destroyed and can even become a biohazard if too many nitrates build up.

- **Residue.** The growing process leaves residue on plants. Even organic farmers have to beware of their fertilizer; if managed improperly it can harbor pathogens that can make you sick. Conventional farmers face a different kind of risk. Although we know that the current sprays used on food are fairly harmless in comparison to naturally occurring pesticides (with the possible exception of Round-Up), repeated applications multiply the impact. At the same time, if bioengineering companies win out, these chemicals will get stronger and stronger and more and more will be used. We don't need to add a greater burden to our already taxed immune systems.

- **Workers.** Farms are not isolated organisms. Armies of low-paid workers, most often from Central and South America, support most big farms. These people are not protected and have fewer rights than the rest of us. If they don't come here, we often bring the farm to them, establishing large industrial farms in Mexico, where we feel free to pollute their environment instead of ours. The National Cancer Institute has been conducting an agricultural health study on farms using pesticides since 1993 and profiling 90,000 people from the Midwest. Farmers and their wives are less likely to get heart disease, but are much more likely to get all kinds of cancer, including leukemia, lymphoma, myeloma, sarcoma, stomach cancer, prostate cancer, and brain cancer. The NCI also studied twenty different common chemicals and their effects and found evidence that for many of them the risk of certain cancers doubled over years of farm exposure. We have a very small population of farmers who are aging rapidly, and they are shortening their life spans even more with each application of pesticides.

- **The future.** The future of food frightens many people. Economists wonder how we'll feed everyone with our current system. With imports and exports so important to our economic well-being today, it scares them silly to think of growing everything locally. An organic system is believed to be less efficient. However, economists don't think about the other costs: environmental, health, or human rights. These costs aren't included in the price of food because they are intangible.

We are so distant from our food that it is difficult to remember these problems when were are not faced with them directly. Who are the people who feed us every day? In Argentina, a beautiful baby girl was born to Sofia Gatica in 1999. Just three days later Sofia lost her perfect child to mysterious kidney failure. Devastated, Sofia was determined to find out why, and she embarked on a relentless pursuit for justice. She began talking to her neighbors in the farming community of Ituzaingó, Argentina, which exports 30 million tons of soybeans every year. The soybean fields surrounding their homes have been sprayed with pesticides for decades and that has had a deadly impact. Sofia's informal survey showed that their small community suffered a much higher occurrence of health problems, including a cancer rate 41 percent higher than the national average. Years passed and she and her band of steadfast mothers continued to fight for truth amidst death threats and harassment until the government finally took notice. The University of Buenos Aires conducted a study that confirmed her results, and an ordinance was finally passed creating a buffer zone around residences. Chemicals could no longer be sprayed within one and a half miles. This small victory only fueled their battle against glyphosate, and these Mothers of Ituzaingó won't be happy until Round-Up is completely banned in Argentina.

These same soybeans from Argentina have been grown for years to feed the cattle that make our hamburgers. The question is, how many people are we willing to kill to eat a cheaper hamburger? Is it fine for one Argentinean baby to die? Is it acceptable for a Midwestern farmer's life to be cut short?

One of our greatest foibles as humans is to say we support something, tell everyone about it, and then do nothing. This is a bad habit that is perpetuated daily on Facebook. A thousand people will post a link about the benefits of buying and eating organic food, but very few are growing it themselves. The greatest action we can take against this catastrophe is to grow some food. Even if you live in a home with no patio and only one window, you can still grow *something*.

We know the basic principles: the soil, composting, seeds, and the philosophy behind organic growing. But, there are a few more strategies to help you be successful:

1. Placement
2. Protection
3. Prevention

Placement

The placement of crops in organic growing is one of the most important considerations. It involves knowing the lay of the land and what else is growing nearby. Each plant has its own specific needs for soil type, water, sun, and temperature, and the environment you provide can mean the difference between a healthy plant and no plant at all. So, the first thing to do is map out your garden space. What are your lowest and highest temperatures every year? What kinds of soils do you have? Where do you get the most sun?

Raised bed or container gardening will be vastly more successful for you than tilling and row-cropping. Raised beds prevent all kinds of pests from getting access to your plants, help with drainage, and are perfect for no-till soil care. Container gardening can be even better because it deters all kinds of burrowing beetles and creatures, and you can move the containers around year to year to confuse other pests.

Once you've placed your beds in the warmest, sunniest spot and filled them with perfect soil (remember everything you learned in the first chapter?), you now have to decide on the placement of each plant species. This is where crop rotation comes in. Crop rotation is a strategy of moving plants around to make sure the soil does not get tired out or depleted and to confuse pests who tend to return to the same spot every year. This plan always includes a legume that returns nitrogen to the soil, and big farms will often rotate alfalfa or clover, but you can use peas or beans, as well. So, every year, at least once, you must grow a legume in every square inch of soil. By returning nitrogen to the soil, the legume is doing a job that would require lots of fertilizer instead, but it does this without energy, without cost, and you might get some food out of it, too.

The next part of crop rotation requires an understanding of some of the basic vegetable families. The "Everything else" category includes plants that don't belong in a whole family, but have their own rotation.

Alliums: the onion and garlic family

Brassicas: the cabbage family, including Brussels sprouts, kohlrabi, kale, pak choi, arugula, turnips, and rutabagas

Chenopodiacaea: the beet family, including Swiss chard and spinach

Cucurbits: the cucumber, melon, and squash family

Legumes: peas and beans

Solanaceae: tomatoes, peppers, potatoes, and eggplants

Umbeliferae: the carrot family, including cilantro, dill, parsley, parsnip, and fennel

Everything else: mint, oregano, rosemary, sage, basil, berry fruit, lettuce, endive, cress, Jerusalem artichoke, corn, and asparagus

Imagine you have a little garden bed. In that bed you decide to grow spinach, which takes only a couple of months to grow. Once it's done, what do you grow next? You can't grow beets or Swiss chard because they are from the same family, so you need to choose from another family. You predict that you can grow at least one more crop in the heat of summer before cold weather hits. Spinach does not feed heavily from the soil and is not prone to many problems, so you can follow it up with most other plants. It's a good idea to grow brassicas right after growing peas because they need a lot of nitrogen. Carrots prefer cooler weather, so a good choice to follow the spinach crop might be bunching onions, squash, or even tomatoes depending on the length of the growing season. Then sow peas at the end of the year. Between each planting it's important to also add an inch of rich compost. For tomatoes you can add a little more.

Most of us grow more than one type of vegetable at a time, and so this is where *companion planting* comes in. Some plants do better next to other plants and knowing which are beneficial and which are harmful can help stave off pests. Some people really take this to extremes, but just understanding plant families and knowing a few rules is enough. It's safe to say that a plant can grow next to one from its own family, but it's also a good strategy to space them out if possible because they are susceptible to the same pests. If you move them away from each other one is more likely to survive.

Companion Plants

Type	Friends	Enemies
Alliums	Umbeliferae	
Asparagus	Umbeliferae	Alliums Solanaceae
Beans	Cucurbits	Brassicas Alliums
Beets	Brassicas Alliums	Legumes

Brassicas	Dill	Solanaceae
	Rosemary	Potato
Carrots	Alliums	Dill
	Radish	
Corn	Cucurbits	Solanaceae
Cucurbits	Nasturtium	Brassicas
	Radish	Basil
		Potato
Lettuce	Radish	Beans
	Cucurbits	Chenopodiacaea
Potato	Beans	Cucurbits
	Corn	Raspberries
	Brassicas	
Solanaceae	Beans	Brassicas
	Spinach	
	Garlic	
Spinach	Radish	
	Strawberry	
	Solanaceae	

Many of these companion plants can also be *intercropped,* or planted in between each other. For example, in the crop rotation we talked about earlier, the spinach can be planted with radishes in between, and the bunching onions that follow could eventually have carrots among them, as well. What was originally one crop of spinach is now radishes, carrots, onions, peas, and spinach in the same bed in the same year, which not only increases our chances of getting a good crop, but also increases our yields overall.

Protection

Most professional organic growers use man-made materials to protect their crops, whether that is a massive commercial greenhouse or a plastic sheet thrown on the ground. I hate plastic as much as the next person, but it is a tremendously useful and necessary tool in organic growing. Most people in North America live in a temperate region, with cold, wet winters and hot, dry summers. This climate also provides the perfect home for a variety of molds and pests that don't exist in the desert. We may think people in the south are the only ones who can grow all year-round, but that's not true. Welcome to the miracle of plastic.

There are other ways we can protect our crops, but they all use similar materials. Glass is an obvious choice, but unless you have a bunch of old windows, it is much more expensive. You are more likely to be able to get plastic, and there are two kinds. The first is clear and lightweight and should be 3 micrometers thick (called 3-mil poly at the store). These sheets are for use as "floating row covers," which is just another phrase for the plastic thrown on top of plants at night to prevent frost damage. You can use this cheap stuff to lengthen your growing season by about a month in northern regions, and several months in southern regions. The second type is clear and heavy weight and should be a minimum of 6-mil poly (6 micrometers). This plastic sheeting is used with hoops made of electrical conduit or PVC, which can be built as a low tunnel on each raised bed, or as a big high tunnel or greenhouse out of wood or metal. Depending on the weather, the 6-mil sheeting can be reused a second year, but the 3-mil can't. The heavier plastic can allow you to grow all your crops much earlier in the year. Plastic floating row covers can only help you grow cool-weather crops earlier. They won't protect your plants from snow. For example, you can use the 3-mil floating cover to grow kale into the winter, but with a 6-mil tunnel you can grow carrots, broccoli and other cool-weather crops in the dead of winter.

The other kind of plastic cover is nonwoven polypropylene. It looks like fabric and provides the same frost protection, pest, and temperature control of plastic, but also allows moisture and light in, and it breathes better. This sheeting is used extensively by northern growers and tends to be more expensive than plastic, but is supposed to last longer. It's a good idea to try both in your area and see which you like better. This fabric cover can be used earlier as a low hoop tunnel or as a floating row cover.

The final material is mulch. Organic certification stipulates that you cannot use plastic mulch permanently, because these big plastic sheets begin to degrade over time and add little bits of plastic to the soil. Plastic mulch keeps the weeds down exponentially, reducing labor dramatically, but you have to pull it up every year at least once and do a proper crop rotation. If you do that, plastic mulch can be extremely valuable. The black color warms up the soil earlier, keeps moisture in—which reduces your watering time—and deters burrowing pests. Alternatively, you could use leaves, and bark works very well for pathways. Leaf mulch has the added value of not having to be removed and provides more needed nutrients to the soil, but isn't effective at deterring pests and doesn't stop weeds, as well.

It is likely that as you start out, you may have to prioritize what is protected based on the size of your budget. Your warm weather crops like tomatoes, peppers, and cucumbers need heat in the beginning of the year, and a greenhouse can give it to them. Greens are another crop that is a priority, especially from the brassica family. They are extremely susceptible to pests that hold over from year to year, but if you tuck them in tightly with a fiber floating row cover, you can keep the pests at bay.

Prevention

This is just a reiteration of everything we have talked about regarding organic growing. It starts with composting religiously and repeatedly adding it to the soil every time you grow something. Simply paying attention to what is going on in the dirt goes a long way.

Then we have placement and protection, which are both part of prevention, as well. Prevention is much easier than repair. Once attacked by a pest, a plant has a very difficult time recovering, because some of the energy that would have gone to producing an edible fruit or vegetable now has to go to repair. If you are fraught with fungus and disease, you will have to destroy every plant that is even slightly infected to save the rest. And you can't throw them in your compost pile. It means making hard choices and even when things look like the end of the world, being resolved to never use chemicals. Without step-by-step prevention, organic growing doesn't work.

Weeds are a big problem in the spring. Your tiny vegetable seedlings begin to grow only to be choked out by weeds that grow much faster. Most plants can be transplanted, which not only starts them off earlier, but also gives them a jump on the weeds. Beans, corn, cucurbits, mustard, peas, and turnips are the few plants that are not worth transplanting, but everything else can be planted in flats or trays according to the directions on the packet. As the time approaches for them to be planted outside, they need to be *hardened off*. This just means getting them used to the outside environment. As the weather warms up, bring them outside to a sheltered place like a porch during the day for longer and longer periods of time, a couple hours the first day, a few the next, and by the end of the week they can be out all day and night. Remove them from the seedling trays without disturbing the roots and pop them into the ground so that the soil comes up almost to the first leaves. This helps them establish their root base faster.

If you have prepared the soil properly, it will be full of compost and should sit at a nice even 6.0 or 6.5 on the pH scale, with not too much of anything. However, some plants like broccoli and tomatoes use so many nutrients during the season that they need a kick. Kelp tea is the easiest way to do this. You can buy liquid kelp, or make your own tea by buying kelp meal or gathering fresh kelp from the ocean. Soak the kelp in water for a couple weeks and pour it directly on the plants. Neem and alfalfa powder can be mixed in for an even more potent tea. This will boost your plants' vitality and help keep their immune systems strong.

Even if you decide that you can't grow very much food, knowing how food is grown organically will help you to know your farmer's practices better and make better choices. Your best defense is knowledge.

CHAPTER FIVE

Undercover Agents

"There are two things you don't want to see being made: sausage and legislation."

—Otto von Bismark

The Food Safety Modernization Act

"The history of government regulation of food safety is one of government watchdogs chasing the horse after it's out of the barn."

—FDA Commissioner David A. Kessler, M.D.

In 2009, the enactment of a key piece of legislation created an email hysteria. The introduction of the Food Safety Modernization Act (or FSMA) spawned rumors that people's backyard gardens were under threat and organic food would be required to be sprayed with pesticides. Of course, neither of those things turned out to be true. It was created to begin the first overhaul of food safety policy in seventy years. This piece of legislation was intended to prevent large processors and industrial farms, such as meat-packing facilities processing thousands of head of cattle each day, from harboring dangerous pathogens by holding them accountable for better preventative measures and detailed and traceable record keeping. It effectively gave the FDA power to impose higher standards for domestic and imported foods and finally gave them power to order recalls.

However, if we are talking about small farms and local food security, the FSMA failed miserably. While large producers have the cash flow to purchase equipment upgrades and pay more office staff to manage detailed paperwork, small farms don't, and if they didn't comply with any of the FDA's forthcoming regulations, they could be forced out of business. Eventually an amendment was added that allowed farms that sold directly to consumers to be exempt from some of the new requirements if they provided documentation to the FDA. This included allowing low-risk foods processed at home to continue to be sold at the farmers' market, a grant program to educate farmers on food safety, and a limit on the amount of record keeping they would have to maintain if they made under a certain amount of money. The record-keeping component is one of the major costs to small farmers, as tracing every item from field to table takes more labor, and labor is the major expense of a small farm. Previously, it was not a priority for small farms to be "traceable," but this new crackdown made small farms part of the paper trail. The FDA says it has done this to protect small farms from being sued by people who could get salmonella or E. coli, and this seems like a legitimate concern. According to the USDA, salmonella is the most common food-borne illness and contaminated eggs cause between 650,000 and *3.8 million* cases of salmonella each year. There was a time that eggs could be eaten raw without concern, and your grandparents made their own mayonnaise and eggnog without worrying, so what changed? The FDA and USDA are slow to pinpoint the culprit, but the European Union is not.

A comprehensive study instituted by the EU and carried out by the European Food Safety Authority compared battery-caged (cages smaller than a piece of paper), cage-free, organic, and free-range eggs. They found a clear winner in the fight against salmonella. Cage-free production cut down salmonella by almost half, and free-range production cut contamination down by 98 percent. As a result, the European Union banned battery cages and saw a huge decline in salmonella outbreaks.

Small farms don't keep their hens in battery cages, and thus have an extremely low risk of salmonella poisoning, yet North American regulations treat every farm the same. Rather than fixing the underlying cause of illness, both the FDA and USDA would rather cater to corporations, whose bottom line is directly affected by the way chickens are kept. Instead of simply banning battery cages, they create more and more ineffective sanitary measures and paperwork. These include more effectively controlling rodents, cleaning out the barn if an egg tests positive for salmonella, and keeping better records so that eggs can be traced to their source barn.

The irony of this is that as of this writing, besides all the record-keeping requirements, the FDA has only created regulations for two products under the FSMA: sprouts and milk. The FSMA simply makes it a requirement that there be more regulations in specific food categories but doesn't say in what way. It is hypocritical in its shortsightedness. The regulations that the FDA has managed to put in place regarding sprouts and milk only affect the small producers, not the big ones. The FDA issued warnings to the public to avoid all raw sprouts if they want to avoid salmonella (simultaneously devastating the small sprout producer industry), and created strict licensing rules. Sprout producers must be licensed as Retail Food Establishments, even when selling directly to the public, which is the same license required to become a restaurant, and wholly impractical for the small grower. At the same time the FDA banned all raw milk (milk that has not been pasteurized).

Pasteurization is the process of heating milk to just below boiling temperature for a short time, and then cooling it down quickly. The goal is to kill disease-causing pathogens that can be introduced to milk after it comes out of the cow and makes contact with many different surfaces. Pasteurization also has the additional benefit of increasing the shelf life of milk by several weeks. You can do this easily at home if you have a cow that is producing more milk than you can drink right away. Unfortunately this process changes the taste and kills good bacteria in the milk as well.

The pathogens that milk can carry are quite serious, just like any other food. According to the Centers for Disease Control (CDC), over a ten-year span (1998–2008), raw milk made 2,000 people sick, or an average of 200 people a year. Two out of these 2,000 people got a disease that paralyzed them for the rest of their lives. Two more people died. However, in 2007 the CDC conducted a raw milk survey and discovered that 3 percent of the population is drinking it. This means that more than 9 million people consume raw milk regularly. From the two reports, we may conclude that .02 percent will get sick, and .00002 percent will die from drinking raw milk.

According to the CDC, milk caused 4,700 illnesses over a thirteen-year period (1993–2006), and state officials determined that 2,800 of them were caused by raw milk. Unfortunately they don't say how they determined this, but let's accept their numbers just for the sake of argument. This leaves 1,900 cases that were caused by pasteurized milk, but nonetheless the CDC concluded that getting sick from raw milk was much more likely to send you to the hospital. While most Americans drink more soda than milk, about 75 percent of the population drinks milk regularly, especially children. This means that of the 234 million pasteurized dairy consumers, .0000004 percent get sick. The fact remains that even though the chances are small, you are more likely to die from raw milk than you are to get sick from pasteurized milk. What government regulators have failed to point out is that the kind of raw milk, and where it comes from, makes a huge difference. A Mexican soft cheese called queso fresco, for example, caused many of the illnesses from raw milk cited by the CDC. The CDC lumped together the cases of poisoning from the large Hispanic population that makes this cheese at home from raw milk, often in bathtubs.

With all the concern over raw milk, why isn't there similar worry about raw beef? Every year, 25,000 people are infected with E. coli in the United States, a terrible illness caused by fecal matter in our food, most commonly in our undercooked beef. The first sign is diarrhea that can quickly escalate to organ failure and even death. The chance of contracting this infection is .01 percent, only slightly better than for raw milk. And yet we are free to buy and cook our steak how we see fit and order medium-rare hamburgers at restaurants, even though these same restaurants warn us to eat meat that is fully cooked.

Prior to the FDA's ban on raw milk, sales were not federally regulated, and the rules were formed on a state or provincial level. Twenty-eight states had allowed farmers to sell raw milk, or milk that had not been pasteurized, and many other states and provinces allowed customers to purchase a "cow share," or a piece of ownership in the cow if the milk itself wasn't legal. For the small farmer, the prohibitive cost of pasteurizing that milk himself means he must sell it to a distributor. However, the quantity that these small farms produce isn't usually enough to make it worthwhile or profitable for the distributor, which leaves the small farmer without the means to pasteurize his milk even if he wanted to. In the United States, if you produce enough milk, you can earn a government subsidy. This means that the larger producers have the added advantage of being able to undercut the small farms on price. It's even worse in Canada, where raw milk has been banned since 1991. If a farmer has more than one cow, he can get into trouble with the provincial milk boards, which by law require that the farmer own a quota. The federal government sets a national quota on milk, and this is divided among the provinces, which is then divided among farms. A milk quota costs about $20,000 to $40,000 *per cow*, and most dairy farmers need to have seventy cows to make a living.

The FDA (and the Canadian Food and Drug Regulations) has made it impossible for a small scale, local milk supply to exist legally in North America. In Europe, raw milk is legal with proper labeling ("Lait Cru" or "unpasteurized milk"). In France, unpasteurized dairy is considered the best and most sacred kind. Vending machines in urban centers even dispense fresh raw milk, and French raw milk cheeses aged less than sixty days are a prized addition to any fine meal. A secretive underground trade even exists to bring French raw milk Camembert from Canada into the United States in small quantities for "personal use," utilizing a loophole in the less-strict cheese rules of Canada.

We take health risks every day. People who purchase raw milk do so for the health benefits and to support local small farms. I make no claim about the health benefits of raw milk, which its supporters say relieves lactose intolerance and provides beneficial enzymes that aid in digestion. However, I think there are much better reasons why raw milk should be legal.

Small farm milk, like grass-fed beef, is typically from cows raised on pasture. Because of this, just like the eggs of chickens who roam free, it is much less likely to carry diseases passed on from cow to cow than the milk from a large dairy farm. According to the CDC, milk is contaminated by cow feces, udder infection, diseases carried by cows, bacteria living on cows' skin, the environment, and rodents, all of which are multiplied exponentially in a dairy feedlot where cows are packed together and fed corn. Evidence suggests that dairy cows on pasture live longer, rarely fall ill, and produce milk for many more years (Clancy). That said, small farms must adhere to sustained and rigorous sanitation procedures. All milking and storage equipment must be sterilized, and each cow needs to be closely monitored for illness. Prior to this legislation, consumers were generally free to find a trustworthy farmer and buy fresh raw milk. Until the last decade, the relationship between the farmer and the consumer was still a right, not a privilege. Milk is now the first product that small farmers are effectively not allowed to produce. As large corporations destroy our food system more and more, and the FDA and USDA cater to their demands, will farmers be banned from producing other things without prohibitively expensive equipment? This is just beginning. Any law that cuts out the small farmer is actually cutting into our food security and our right to access the food we need.

The Raw Milk Rebellion

"I hold it that a little rebellion now and then is a good thing, and as necessary in the political world as storms in the physical."

—Thomas Jefferson

The raw milk story doesn't end with the advent of legislation. There is a small army of people fighting back and supporting small farms out of principle, and there are farmers who are digging in their heels and selling raw milk regardless of the law. However, the level of government crackdown on these rebels is extreme, sometimes violent, and illustrates a much deeper problem.

The first real target was Richard Hebron in 2006, a farmer and owner of a co-op in Vandalia, Michigan, that distributed eggs, milk, and other farm-fresh goods to the surrounding area. When a couple of children became sick due to a food-borne illness that was suspected to be caused by raw milk (but never confirmed), an expensive investigation began that involved sending in an undercover agent from the Michigan Agricultural Department to purchase raw milk from Hebron's co-op and track his movements. Along with Michigan state police, Agricultural Department agents waited until he was on his way from Vandalia to Ann Arbor, the 140-mile trip he made each week to deliver the milk and other goods, then pulled him over and seized $7,000 worth of raw milk. They simultaneously served his wife with a warrant, seized the couple's computer and business records, and searched their warehouse in Ann Arbor. Raw milk sales were illegal in Michigan, and they were able to confiscate the milk on the grounds of suspected contamination resulting in the possible illness of the children who had contracted a food-borne disease.

Hebron, however, had not produced the milk himself. This milk had come from a farm owned by an Amish farmer named David Hochstetler, from Middleburg, Indiana, who owned seventy cows, and when news of the raid came out, nervous stores in Ann Arbor pulled the plug on the farm's milk. Cow shares, as mentioned earlier, are a way for customers and farmers to circumvent state raw milk legislation. While the sale of raw milk is banned, owning a *share* of a cow is not, and co-ops like Hebron's help distribute raw milk from the farmer to the cow owners, usually through drop-off points at local health food stores and food co-ops. However, federal law prohibits transporting raw milk across state lines, as Hebron was doing when carrying milk from Hochstetler's farm in Indiana.

Fortunately, thousands of concerned citizens emailed government leaders when they heard what had happened to Hebron, and under their intense pressure, the state of Michigan decided to send him just a warning letter about trafficking raw milk across state lines. Hebron was served a $1,000 fine for breaking some egg and meat processing regulations. The Hebrons were back in business.

However, this wasn't the end of the story. The Amish farmer, David Hochstetler, continued to sell raw milk through the cow-share loophole. But when an outbreak of campylobacteriosis (an infection commonly contracted from many kinds of foods) in Michigan occurred in 2010, the FDA decided to use this as a reason to target Hochstetler's farm. They arrived unannounced, wanting to inspect and test his milk. Hochstetler called Sheriff Brad Rogers, the local law enforcement officer, and Rogers decided to uphold Hochstetler's right to protection from unwarranted searches. Sheriff Rogers told federal agents that if they stepped foot on the property without a warrant, he would arrest them.

Meanwhile, Hochstetler had his milk independently tested and found it to be perfectly clean. In effect, Hochstetler had lost thousands of gallons of milk in the previous Hebron raid (and thousands of dollars), and endured federal harassment for years, for no good reason. His cows had never made anyone sick.

As of today, the case against Hebron and Hochstetler remains unresolved. The Michigan Department of Agriculture and the FDA continue to state that they may or may not issue a warrant in the future and will continue their investigation. While his peers gave Sheriff Rogers a "Meritorious Valor" award for upholding the Constitution, the federal government felt quite differently. Federal agents have continued to attempt to step onto Hochstetler's property, and in November 2011 he was subpoenaed to appear before a grand jury in connection with the outbreak of illness, to which he had supposedly been linked by the FDA. However, the next month he received a letter that the subpoena had been withdrawn. The high level of support for Hochstetler and Hebron, including free representation by top lawyers, has temporarily kept the FDA at bay, but for how long?

In 2009 another Amish farmer was the victim of an FDA sting operation. Dan Allgyer sold cow shares in Pennsylvania and distributed raw milk in Maryland to the suburbs. The FDA went undercover, purchasing a share and having the milk delivered to Washington, D.C. (Isn't it interesting that the FDA is willing to go undercover to investigate Amish dairy farms, and yet it is animal rights groups that must go undercover to investigate factory farms?)

In April 2010, the FDA filed an injunction on Allgyer accusing him of selling raw milk. Just before dawn they staged a surprise raid and confiscated hundreds of gallons of milk, launching a two-year long legal battle. Finally, the court ordered a permanent injunction against Allgyer. In February 2012, Allgyer made the decision to shut down the farm after the terrible stress the ordeal had placed on his family.

Meanwhile, in Canada, Michael Schmidt fared no better. In November 2006, twenty-five heavily armed officers raided his Ontario farm. They confiscated milk, computers, and equipment, and he received a court order to stop selling raw milk in compliance with Canadian law. By September 2008, he was found to be in contempt of court. He also faced other serious charges from the local health authority and the Ministry of Natural Resources. He represented himself in court in January 2010 and happily won an acquittal on all nineteen charges. However, the fight wasn't over yet. The government appealed the decision, and in September 2011 he was found guilty in Ontario Court of selling raw milk on fifteen of the nineteen original charges.

Schmidt fought back, starting a hunger strike that lasted a month. After losing fifty pounds, he finally agreed to break his strike when Ontario Premier Dalton McGuinty decided to meet with him. His first meal was, appropriately, a glass of raw milk, but in November 2011 he was still sentenced to one year of probation and a $9,000 fine for the fifteen charges of which he was found guilty. He countered with an appeal, but as of this writing, this case has still not gone back to court. Schmidt even faced a contempt of court charge in British Columbia, as well, for helping the Home on the Range dairy farm co-op in Chilliwack, British Columbia. Fortunately, that hearing was "indefinitely postponed."

As if things couldn't be more insane, his story took an interesting twist in August 2012, when police and the Canadian Food Inspection Agency raided his farm for a second time, seizing phones and computers in a search that lasted eight hours. The search warrant was in connection with the theft of thirty rare, previously mentioned Shropshire sheep that had been stolen from Wholearth Farmstudio in April. The sheep were recovered in June, on a farm thirty minutes from Schmidt's farm. The recovered sheep tested negative for scrapie, but were killed despite being clean. Although no charges were laid, the warrant accused Schmidt of conspiracy to obstruct inspectors and removing animals from a quarantined farm, which is a criminal offence.

There are many more stories like these, and if it seems as though the violence is increasing, it is. In June 2010, a heavily armed police team raided a Venice, California, raw food cooperative called Rawsome after a year-long sting operation. They dumped all the raw milk on the premises, confiscated all the cash in the till, and took hundreds of pounds of fresh produce. Then they arrested one of the owners, James Stewart, allegedly without presenting a warrant or reading him his rights. Stewart and the other two owners,

Sharon Palmer and Eugenie Bloch, faced serious criminal charges related to conspiracy to sell raw milk.

What is immediately interesting about this case is that selling raw milk is legal for retail stores in California that have obtained a license. Rawsome never had one and didn't even have a business license during the six years they were in operation because they weren't a store. As a food-buying club, members paid a fee to be able to enter the warehouse, and the workers were all volunteers, so it was never a retail establishment. Trying to convince the state of California how a food cooperative works proved impossible, however, as many of the charges are based on the premise that Rawsome was a retail store operating without a license.

There are those who argue that the state has been more than generous in allowing raw milk sales to continue as long as sellers have a license, and it was Rawsome's own fault for not complying with the red tape. Rawsome's security camera footage captures police entering with their guns drawn. This seems a bit drastic for a simple licensing issue. Later, Stewart, Palmer, and Bloch were arrested a second time for continuing to distribute raw milk, after a second raid in August 2011. This second raid involved the FDA, FBI, and local police, and this time law enforcement officials were smart enough to disable the security cameras. These three were released on $30,000 bail each and are still facing trial as of this writing.

Let's backtrack a little . . .

Looking at all the problems small farmers are facing, can we truly call food production in North America democratic? It doesn't seem so. The raw milk issue is just one in a series of oppression-by-legislation measures. Small grain producers have no protection from genetic drift and Monsanto. Organic papaya farmers in Hawaii are disappearing. Small dairies are being forced to shut down. In Canada, eggs, meat, milk, potatoes, tomatoes, peppers, cucumbers, onions, turnips, cabbage, and butter lettuce can't be legally grown unless the farmer owns a quota, which has forced out many small farmers, and those who grow them anyway can be raided and lose everything.

Food legislation is constantly revised with measures that repress the small farmer. On one hand the government promotes "local food," but on the other it acts to squash any small farmer who is even mildly financially successful. It's a sick game, and everyone loses. It is conceivable that in the near future growers may not be permitted to sell their produce at farmers' markets without more licenses, and that more limits to production will be introduced to keep small farms unprofitable. We might think that no one will be willing to enforce such rules, but as we can see from the raw milk raids, this is already happening.

Battle for Urban Farms

"You do not examine legislation in the light of the benefits it will convey if properly administered, but in the light of the wrongs it would do and the harms it would cause if improperly administered."

—Lyndon B. Johnson

In July 2011, Julie Bass of Oak Park, Michigan, decided to create an educational and useful project for her six children. When the front of her yard was torn up because of sewer repairs, she decided to build five raised garden beds instead of replacing the lawn. They were neat and tidy and surrounded by bark mulch. Not only did her children love growing vegetables, her neighbors also loved walking by and chatting with her about all the beautiful food they were growing.

That was until the city took notice and slapped her with a warning to remove the garden because it violated city bylaws. The city said that according to the ordinance, all front yard plants must be "suitable"—and for some reason vegetables are not—despite there being no clear definition of what *suitable* means. Rather than bow down to the powers that be, she refused and was charged with a misdemeanor. She faced a maximum sentence of ninety-three days in jail. Fortunately she also gained a bit of fame, which brought attention to her cause. After months of harassment from city hall, the fallout from the media became so massive that government officials began to cave. Eventually they dropped the illegal garden charges and then tried to charge Julie with a dog license violation before finally giving up. She wrote on her blog, "I just went along, figuring that most rules had good reasons, and I was mostly happy to comply. But this entire experience has shown me that you have to be educated. You have to ask questions. You have to have a strong internal compass for morality, and you have to be willing to stand by your Self (capital S on purpose) even in the face of people standing against you."

Julie's just one of many gardeners who have taken a stand against municipal bureaucracy. In 2010, a Georgia man was fined $5,200 for growing "too many" vegetables. Steve Miller had been growing vegetables for fifteen years on his one-and-a-half-acre plot. He had filled his yard with crops that he sold at farmers' markets or gave away to friends. He never realized that the zoning for his land allowed for backyard gardens and not urban agriculture, but the lines between those two things are often very fuzzy. The county agreed to rezone his property, but he was still liable for the fine.

In 2011, Novella Carpenter faced an urban farm crackdown from the city of Oakland, California. She eyed the empty lot next to her house every day with big ideas of growing food, until one day she just did it. Later she bought the property, but it was after that point that the city caught on and charged her with illegal agricultural activities (selling excess produce without a permit), carrying a fine of $5,000. If she didn't stop farming, they would allow her to continue, if she paid $2,500 for a Conditional Use Permit. She paid for the permit.

In British Columbia, the bureaucrats in the rural town of Lantzville had a real problem with farmer Dirk Becker. Becker's Compassion Farm is near my home on Vancouver Island, and everyone knows who he is—a very vocal local food advocate and an energetic force at the farmers' markets. By November 2010, Becker had been farming for twelve years on his 2.5 acres, located in a rural area where almost everyone owns acreage. One day after receiving his regular load of composted horse manure, a troublesome neighbor complained about the smell to the city bylaw enforcement (this despite the many horses kept on many other properties in the nearby vicinity). Officers arrived to inspect the property and were surprised to discover that Becker was growing commercially on a property zoned as residential. They ordered Becker to stop farming commercially, but Becker rallied the community and garnered international publicity. However, the city council and the mayor became more and more stubborn in their approach. They required him to sign an order that would stop him from importing any more horse manure. Then they ordered him to stop selling rain barrels. Eventually they ordered him to stop farming, or at least apply for a temporary use permit to continue farming until a committee could discuss a revised plan. Becker refused to stop farming and rejected an offer for a temporary use permit. He stated in a press release, "Urban Farming is a global movement and is moving past being 'allowed' or 'permitted' to being supported, encouraged and protected." The city advised him to hire a lawyer, as he could be facing six months in jail, and then created an urban garden committee made up of several city council members and a few locals to "discuss" the issue, but never consulted Becker or any other urban farmers. The committee met privately over the course of a couple of months and issued a final report in October 2011, which was met with a great deal of dissatisfaction by supporters of Becker's farm. The report outlined that it was reasonable to limit urban food gardens to 30 percent of the property space, and that animal manure could not be used as fertilizer. Both of these stipulations would be a serious handicap for Becker's farm.

This went on for more than a year, with Becker claiming ongoing harassment from the neighbor and letters from the city that threatened further legal action. But when Mayor Haime came up for reelection, the voters made their choice and Haime was ousted at the end of 2011. He had this to say: "You supported an individual who thumbed his nose up at the bylaws of the community and its residents including his neighbour. You have set the precedent whereby laws are now set by conflict. The loudest one wins. At the same time you abandoned and ridiculed law abiding citizens who were only interested in the piece (sic) and enjoyment of their own property. You want the right to do as you please but you deny the rights of others the same thing."

At the same time, the town of Lantzville successfully amended their bylaw to allow urban food gardens with a variety of requirements and even organized a new farmers' market. Today, Lantzville has a vibrant local food community run by the Friends of Urban Agriculture Lantzville (without any involvement by Becker at all), who advocate for improved bylaws on an ongoing basis.

In Jacksonville, Florida, residents are allowed to have a few laying hens in their backyard, for the high price of $750. The fee was established thirty years prior as a way of allowing people to have horses within city limits, but the language was so vague that the fee now applies to any farm animal. Citizens are refusing to pay, but the fine for having rogue chickens is in the thousands of dollars. The community has provided tremendous support for changing the bylaw, but the process is exhaustive and very, very slow. This situation is mirrored in most towns in North America, and as more people grow their own food, these battles become more common.

In October 2011, Denise Morrison of Tulsa, Oklahoma, came home one day to find that her edible garden had been completely destroyed. Her suburban oasis had more than a hundred varieties of plants, many of which were medicinal to treat her arthritis and diabetes. She had created the garden after she lost her job and her health insurance, and it was her primary source of food. There were flowers, grapes, strawberries, mint, and even apple, walnut, and pecan trees. Morrison, was shocked but knew exactly who had done it. A few months earlier she had received a letter from the city of Tulsa indicating that there had been a complaint about her yard. This did not trouble her too much, however, because she had been very careful to comply with city code, which states that plants can't be more than twelve inches tall unless they are edible. She took pictures of her yard and met with city inspectors, but when they were unhelpful, she asked them to come to her house and point out where the problems were. It was inconceivable to her that the whole yard could be a problem, but they told her she needed to rip out everything. She got news that they wanted to cut it all down, so she called the police. The officer issued a citation so that it could go to court. In August she went to court, but the judge told her to come back in October. At this point city officials took matters into their own hands and when she was away they cut down the fruit trees and ripped out all her front gardens. She just sat down in her driveway and sobbed.

As of 2012, Morrison has filed a civil lawsuit against the city, but despite the media coverage, it is questionable what kind of solution she will find there. Any real changes in the city's policies or behavior will not happen unless there is a change in leadership.

The most serious and heart-wrenching story of all is the tale of South Central Farm, which has been the subject of a moving documentary called *The Garden*. South Central Los Angeles is not known for its greenery. It is an industrial area filled with concrete and crime. From 1994 to 2006, a fourteen-acre plot of empty land became one of the largest community farms in the United States, providing 350 low-income families with the ability to grow their own fresh food. What had been filled with garbage became a thriving urban garden, growing more than 150 species of plants, some of which were rare and medicinal varieties from Mesoamerica. Originally, nine investors owned the property. In 1986, the city of Los Angeles purchased the property by eminent domain for $4.8 million, which means it forced the sale to build a waste incinerator. When citizens opposed the project, however, the incinerator was never built and the property was sold to the L.A. Regional Food Bank to be used as a community garden.

According to the laws of eminent domain, however, if the city project doesn't go through and the city decides to sell, the original owner is supposed to be given the first opportunity to buy it back. In 2001, one of the original investors, Ralph Horowitz, sued the city for failing to honor that clause, and in 2003 the city sold it back to him for $5 million in a private session without informing or consulting with the public. Since the Food Bank abandoned their project shortly after this deal was made, it is likely that they were aware of this negotiation. In January 2004 Horowitz issued a notice that the South Central gardeners had to remove their belongings by February 29th. However, the newly created South Central Farmers Feeding Families fought back. They were issued a restraining order and threatened with forced eviction. At the same time Horowitz offered to sell the property back to them for $16 million, three times its value, if the sale was completed by May 22nd, less than three months away. The farmers occupied the land continuously in peaceful protest, raised more than $6 million (more than the original price) to buy the land back, but didn't manage to raise the remaining $10 million. On June 7th, the private nonprofit Annenberg Foundation offered the rest of the money, but Horowitz ignored it since it came after his deadline.

By this time the farm was supported and occupied by celebrities like Tom Morello and Serge from the band System of a Down, Daryl Hannah, Joan Baez, Martin Sheen, and Willie Nelson, and the story was unfolding to millions of people across America through the evening news. The overwhelming support was for the farmers. On June 13th the police arrived at the farm and gave the occupants fifteen minutes to leave. Forty people were arrested, including Daryl Hannah who had been camping there for the past three weeks. She had to be removed from a walnut tree. Horowitz stated that he would not sell to the South Central farmers for any price, citing anti-Semitism: "Even if they raised $100 million, this group could not buy this property. It's not about money. It's about I don't like their cause and I don't like their conduct. So there's no price I would sell it to them for" (Ballon). The land was bulldozed while supporters watched, with tears streaming down their cheeks, holding each other, as orchards of fruit and nut trees and years of hard work were destroyed.

Today the land sits empty, despite Horowitz's claims that he would soon be building something there. The South Central Farmers continue to fight for the land, hold candlelight vigils, and have refused to give up. The City did give them three acres to use for a CSA and small-scale community garden, but they still want their original fourteen acres back.

All these battles, even those within the local food movement, represent a growing trend. Food gardens have become a subversive act, because a large majority people in North America live within the jurisdiction of a city bylaw. More than 80 percent of the US population is urban. These bylaws were created with the best of intentions, but they are often woefully outdated. Decades ago, this legislation protected city dwellers from diseases that spread quickly and could have easily been prevented through good hygiene. Often these diseases were linked to having farm animals in the city. However, with today's modern gardening and farming technology, small-scale urban and suburban farms are a responsible way to grow food without causing an epidemic. This kind of babysitting-by-bylaw tactic is no longer necessary.

Organic is Too Expensive

I had strict criteria for the farms that I wanted to research, but not unreasonable demands. They had to be financially independent, use organic standards (but not necessarily have certification), and they must be willing to share everything about their farm. I needed to know their income per square foot, how much debt they had as an operation, and their revenue streams. How was the farm supported? What did it grow or raise? Not only did I want it to be an amazing photographic journey, I wanted to get down to the realities of farming. The farms that responded to my call were of all different types: community farms, individually owned farms, leased land, urban farms, large commercial farms, and ecovillages. They raised all kinds of crops and animals, and marketed their products in every way possible. However, out of hundreds of potentially wonderful farms, only twenty-one made it to my short list as economically viable.

One farm was eliminated because it turned out that their major income came from selling house plants. Out of the remaining twenty, only eight supported their families with solely agricultural-related activities. A working spouse supported the other twelve farms. The eight remaining farms each had its own strategy for survival:

- One was extensively dependent on government grant money at the time.

- One was located on rented farmland near an urban center.

- Several were dependent on speaking engagements and writing income.

- One sold a value-added product (a processed food item).

- One sold to an organic conglomerate (a brand-name label sold in stores).

- Several were dependent on agritourism (like a B&B or camp).

Twelve of the farms were vegetable market farms. Five sold both meat and vegetables. One sold cheese, one was a large dairy farm, and two just produced meat. Almost half had organic certification.

I wanted farms that sold food products only, had no debt, and were the primary financial supporter of the farmer's family. I was forced to conclude that out of the twenty, only one could be defined as a successful farm in the strictest sense according to the guidelines I had set.

I did eventually have some wonderful conversations with several farms. Two of them definitely wanted to share all the knowledge they had, mostly because they wanted to give young people a harsh dose of reality. Two other farms were located near where I live and were going to be our first stop. Unfortunately, none of the farms was willing to take the further step of filling out my much-needed survey to provide me with more details about farm operations.

I was forced to face an uncomfortable fact: The reason that so many farms failed to meet my reasonable criteria, or even contact me, was because the farmers who ran them were doing it as a lifestyle choice rather than as a way to become food suppliers. This generalization may sound unfair, but most organic farmers I spoke to had become organic farmers because of some romantic ideal, had gotten into debt for property and equipment, and now they had to sell their food products at high prices to pay for it.

A Few Model Food Policies

"Today, local economies are being destroyed by the 'pluralistic,' displaced, global economy, which has no respect for what works in a locality. The global economy is built on the principle that one place can be exploited, even destroyed, for the sake of another place."

—Wendell Berry

Maine

People who live in Maine seem to be pretty advanced when it comes to food activism. When the Food Safety Modernization Act was introduced in 2009, Maine citizens immediately took action. Several towns cooperated together to preemptively draft a Local Food and Self-Governance Ordinance. The ordinance states:

We the People of the Town of (name of town), (name of county) County, Maine have the right to produce, process, sell, purchase and consume local foods thus promoting self-reliance, the preservation of family farms, and local food traditions. We recognize that family farms, sustainable agricultural practices, and food processing by individuals, families and non-corporate entities offers stability to our rural way of life by enhancing the economic, environmental and social wealth of our community. As such, our right to a local food system requires us to assert our inherent right to self-government. We recognize the authority to protect that right as belonging to the Town of (name of town).

We have faith in our citizens' ability to educate themselves and make informed decisions. We hold that federal and state regulations impede local food production and constitute a usurpation of our citizens' right to foods of their choice. We support food that fundamentally respects human dignity and health, nourishes individuals and the community, and sustains producers, processors and the environment. We are therefore duty bound under the Constitution of the State of Maine to protect and promote unimpeded access to local foods.

Local Food and Community Self-Governance

The purpose of the Local Food and Community Self-Governance Ordinance is to:

(i). Provide citizens with unimpeded access to local food;

(ii) Enhance the local economy by promoting the production and purchase of local agricultural products;

(iii) Protect access to farmers' markets, roadside stands, farm based sales and direct producer to patron sales;

(iv) Support the economic viability of local food producers and processors;

(v) Preserve community social events where local foods are served or sold;

(vi) Preserve local knowledge and traditional foodways.

They feared, and rightly so, that the Food Safety Modernization Act would be used to prevent the sale of homemade goods at farmers' markets and farm stands. Five towns passed the act right away (Blue Hill, Penobscot, Sedgwick, Trenton, and Hope), but the state immediately retaliated.

On November 9, 2011, Dan Brown of Gravelwood Farm in Blue Hill was served with papers. The state of Maine and Maine Agricultural Commissioner Walter Whitcomb were suing him for selling food and milk without a license, claiming that they had been investigating him for a long time; but the Freedom of Access Act allowed citizens from the grassroots organization Food for Maine's Future to obtain emails detailing the state's true intentions. On April 2, 2011, Blue Hill passed the ordinance, and on June 10th an inspector from the Maine Department of Agriculture visited the Blue Hill Farmers' Market. The inspector informed Farmer Brown that he was in violation of state law by not having licenses for his products.

Brown then told the inspector that he operated under the Local Food & Community Self-Reliance Ordinance, and therefore did not need a license. On June 14th, inspector Jon Morris emailed his report to his superiors at Maine's Quality Assurance and Regulations (QAR), where it was forwarded to various people before QAR Program Manager Steve Guiger forwarded it to his director, Hal Prince, adding, "Sounds like we have our first test case." By choosing a farmer from Local-Food-Ordinance-supporting town of Blue Hill, the state would send a clear message to Maine citizens.

In public statements, the Commissioner and QAR department continued to claim that they had been investigating Dan Brown for years because his products were a significant health risk. The state wanted him to pay fines of $40,000 and stop selling food to anyone, and at the time of this writing the case is still scheduled to go to court. In June 2012, possibly in reaction to the court case, two more Maine towns, Appleton and Livermore, adopted the ordinance. Commissioner Whitcomb responded with a public statement, saying, "The state finds itself in no position to recognize the ordinances."

The food policies in Maine are relatively lenient compared to other states' laws. They allow small farmers to butcher their own chickens for sale rather than sending them to a processing facility, and up until the FSMA was introduced, they were letting farmers sell raw milk as long as it was labeled and sold directly from the farm. Dairy farms must be registered with the state. Farmer Brown, like many Maine farmers who feel that these regulations step on the toes of residents' right to local food, got into trouble when he chose not to comply with any state licensing or registration. In the eyes of Maine citizens who support the food sovereignty ordinances, even their own lenient bureaucracy infringed too much on their rights to grow and sell good food.

Vancouver, British Columbia

The city of Vancouver is not quite as radical as Blue Hill, Maine, but compared to other North American cities, it's far ahead when it comes to local food policies. In July 2003 the city passed a motion to support "the development of a just and sustainable food system." This was defined as a place in which "food production, processing, distribution and consumption are integrated to enhance the environmental, social and nutritional value of a particular place." A food policy task force was created, made of representatives from a variety of city sectors, and together they went through a six-month consultation process with residents, urban farmers, and neighborhood groups. By December they had created an Action Plan with three goals: 1) to create a Vancouver Food Policy Council; 2) to hire two fulltime staff members to facilitate food systems goals; and 3) to immediately begin building rooftop gardens, community gardens, and coordinated food processing and distribution facilities for low-income people.

Since the creation of the council, which meets monthly in an open session at city hall, there have been a number of successful changes. The "Grow a Row, Share a Row" initiative encourages gardeners to grow local produce for the local food bank, an extremely important project that allows people in dire need to receive fresh food rather than nonperishables. The council has amended city bylaws to allow urban beekeeping and has even installed hives on top of city hall. Citizens are now allowed to keep up to four hens for egg production. The city now has seventy-four community gardens with 3,260 plots. Perhaps most importantly, in 2007 the council developed a Vancouver Food Charter, which has five principles:

1. **Community Economic Development.** Supports greater reliance on locally based food systems and their benefits to local and regional economies.
2. **Ecological Health.** Promotes protection of natural resources, reduction of "food miles" *(currently averaging more than 2,500 km from farm to fork)*, reduction of food waste through composting, and enhancement of "edible food recovery."

3. **Social Justice.** Advocates that food is a basic human right and underscores the need of all citizens, and particularly hungry children, for accessible, affordable, healthy, and culturally appropriate food.

4. **Collaboration and participation.** Strengthens food security through citizen engagement and commends cooperation of all levels of government, businesses, and NGOs to promote sound food system strategies.

5. **Celebration.** Promotes the fundamental importance of food in bringing people together for celebration and sharing.

Due largely to the friendly agricultural climate, urban farming in Vancouver has been growing rapidly. By 2010 there were ten commercial urban farms in backyards, on leased government acreage, and even in a parking lot. Altogether the farms used 2.3 acres of land space, but even more incredibly, they employed fifty-one people. In that tiny space, farmers produced $128,500 worth of food (Schutzbank). In 2011, the number of farms was up to fifteen, which means the city's goal to increase the number of farms 400 percent by 2020 might be feasible. The city is still working to eliminate bylaws that inhibit urban farming, but until that point they are turning a blind eye to "illegal" farming activity. Vancouver is in a race to become one of the greenest cities in the world, with its Greenest City 2020 project, and it may very well succeed.

Detroit, Michigan

Most of the stories in this book about Michigan detailing the state's crackdown on vegetable gardens and raw milk raids have been less than positive. There is, however, one place in Michigan that just might be a shining beacon of hope, and that city is Detroit. The city hemorrhaged auto-industry jobs during the recession, losing at least 25 percent of its population during the last ten years. Detroit's economy was so dependent on the auto industry that it had no way to recover. Twenty percent of the houses are now vacant with no one ready to step in and buy them. In 2011, the city made the decision to bulldoze 10,000 empty buildings falling into decay.

Perhaps in an act of desperation, some of the remaining citizens have chosen to save their city by farming. Leading the cause is Greening Detroit, an organization formed in 1989 with the goal of replacing the 500,000 trees that had originally stood where the city was built. Today they are working on urban agriculture and support a network of 10,000 urban gardeners. A study at Michigan State University found that there are more than 4,000 acres of land available in Detroit that could supply 75 percent of the vegetables and 40 percent of the fruit needed by residents. There has not yet been a census on how many urban farms currently exist, but examples abound.

There's Earthworks Urban Farm, a program of the Capuchin Soup Kitchen. It is made up of seven gardens on twenty city lots spread over two blocks (approximately 2.5 acres) producing 7,000 pounds of food each year. There's Edith Floyd, a former school employee who was laid off and had to quickly find a solution to having something to eat. Edith's neighborhood, where she had lived for thirty-seven years, includes sixty-six houses and at one time was a thriving community, but today there are six residents left, three condemned houses, and fifty-seven abandoned homes. As of the end of 2011, Edith has farmed twenty-eight lots. The act of buying up empty lots in Detroit and Cleveland is now called "blotting" rather than squatting. Most of the residents purchase the lots anywhere from $1 to $300 to become the legal owners. Floyd's plan is to just keep on expanding in the hopes of eventually making a profit.

The Detroit Food Policy Council was formed in 2009, with the mission to "nurture the development and maintenance of a sustainable, localized food system and a food-secure City of Detroit in which all of its residents are hunger-free, healthy, and benefit economically from the food system that impacts their lives." The number one goal is to advocate for urban agriculture. Even though the city council seemed supportive and the citizens were pushing for this issue, policy changes were slow in coming, they say, because of the state's Right to Farm Act. This act was created in 1981 as a way of protecting farmers from being sued for noise, smells, dust, or other nuisances. It also included an amendment that prohibits local and city governments from creating any ordinances that might conflict with the act. The city council is concerned that once a farm is created within the city, there would be no way to crack down on ones that might become a nuisance. They say they are trying to create guidelines and limitations to prevent, for example, a pig farmer from settling close to a thriving residential area. At the end of 2011, State Senator Virgil Smith proposed an amendment to the Right to Farm Act specifically exempting the city of Detroit so that the city council could create its own policies. As of this writing, it has not yet been voted on.

One recent setback was the eviction of the Birdtown Community Garden, which had been squatting on an empty lot for seven years through a garden use permit program, but had failed to get the garden permit for the last two years running. It happened to be next door to Canine to Five, a thriving doggy daycare business. When the daycare business wanted to expand, it approached the city about buying the community garden lot, and despite a serious fight from the gardeners and Greening Detroit, the lot sold. City council member Ken Cockrel said, "If we all think about where we want Detroit to go, what we want Detroit to look like, gardening and farming may be important, but the future of this city, we don't want it looking like a farm in Kansas. We want it to look like Chicago. We want it looking like Manhattan. We want it looking like Boston. And that's the bricks and mortar development."

This attitude has caused food policy development in Detroit to stagnate. Fortunately this hasn't stopped farmers like Paul Weertz. He has been blotting for years, and has accumulated ten arable acres of city land on which he raises chickens, bees, fruit trees, alfalfa, and vegetables. Or Caroline Leadley of Rising Pheasant Farms, who owns several plots and grows heirloom vegetables for the farmers' market. The application process to buy land takes eight months, and as Leadley relates, "apparently has to be approved by everyone in

Detroit," so this is a significant accomplishment. Or Greg Willerer of Brother Nature Produce, who grows greens on twelve lots and is also the creator of Detroit Dirt, a composting business. Or Andrew Kemp, who has turned his large acreage into an edible paradise. All these farms are technically illegal because of city policy and could be shut down. It is to the council's credit that only economic development has superseded agricultural activity on urban land.

This policy problem might be about to change, but possibly not for the better. John Hantz, a long-time Detroit resident and millionaire, wants to invest in the future of Detroit by building large farms on abandoned properties. As he has promoted publicly to national media and the city council, he is willing to put in $30 million to convert 250 acres (representing thousands of abandoned homes) into agriculture. His original plan was slated to start development in 2010, but it was delayed because of the city's inability to change zoning or policies. In interviews, Hantz talks about aquaponics and alternative vertical farming, but his real dream is to acquire as much as 10,000 acres of land from the city. The first phase of his proposed project is just to plant trees, though it will eventually move into food crops. The media loves talking about John Hantz as the savior of Detroit. In its profile of Hantz, *Fortune* magazine displayed some editorial idealism: "But allow Hantz to dream a little. Twenty years from now, when people come to the city and have a drink at the bar at the top of the Renaissance Center, what will they see? Maybe that's not the right vantage point. Maybe they'll actually be on the farm, picking apples, looking up at the RenCen. 'That's the beauty of being down and out,' says Hantz. 'You can actually open your mind to ideas that you would never otherwise embrace.' At this point, Detroit doesn't have much left to lose" (Whitford).

The reality of the project isn't lost on its residents, however. Critics believe that this farm project is a land grab, and those familiar with the areas Hantz wants to buy know that he is handpicking land with more commercial development value than other areas. They believe that once he gets what he wants, the farm ruse will be over. It's not a difficult stretch since his proposal doesn't address the possibility of future developments. The city brought in the Detroit City Food Council in November 2011 to discuss finally changing the city's agricultural policies, but Hantz wants to bypass this process and just get the land so he can start growing trees. He didn't care to communicate with the rest of the urban farmers in Detroit. It is disappointing, but not surprising, that his plan is now absent of any mention of food production, and is solely focused on high-value wood products. The project has a new name: Hantz Woodlands Detroit. It is worrying that selfish interests are likely at work to exploit this opportunity. Unfortunately at the end of 2012, Hantz was able to purchase 1,500 lots (about 140 acres of land) for $520,000, far below even Detroit market value.

Detroit's example as a model city comes less from the efforts of the city government and much more from the residents, who are slowly turning desolation into a productive, edible paradise, despite red tape and slow-moving bureaucracy. It will take many years for Detroit to recover from its economic woes, and while the city council still believes this recovery will include a restoration of the city's former glory, it is far more likely to come from farming. Finally, consider the unfortunate news that the Detroit Police Officer's Association recently issued a warning to travelers to stay away from Detroit if they want to avoid violent crime—a partial result of the grossly understaffed police department. As we have seen with other examples in this book, urban farming has been shown to lower crime rates and reduce poverty, neighborhood by neighborhood, and it's time Detroit's City Council embraced that reality.

Seattle, Washington

Seattle didn't need to have a food policy for the city council to embrace urban farming. Urban agricultural initiatives are managed by the Office of Sustainability and Environment, which is heavily involved in facilitating farmers' markets, food bank gardens, and composting. In 2008 the office created the Local Food Action Initiative, which has made huge strides in increasing food security for low-income residents and expanding urban farming. The city helps coordinate community centers as Community Supported Agriculture drop-off sites, including the Seattle Municipal Tower, a sixty-seven-story skyscraper in the heart of downtown. The office has a fruit tree program to help residents maintain and harvest orchards in city parks. It turned a seven-acre nursery into Rainier Beach Urban Farm, now set aside as an education property managed by Seattle Tilth, an organization that has been advocating for organic agriculture for decades. The city also gave forty acres to United People's Farm, a program that partners with Seattle Tilth and Burst for Prosperity, in order to help immigrants, refugees, and other low-income people to build a farm business.

The city council developed the Transfer of Developmental Rights program to protect farmland that specifically supplies produce to Seattle's farmers' markets. In fact, food security and policies are overwhelmingly incorporated into every aspect of city planning, even down to transportation. The Local Food Action Initiative includes these points:

- Define "Community Garden" and allow them outright in all zones.
- Define "Urban Farm" and allow specific appropriate models in each zone.
- Define "Farmers' Markets" as an outright permitted use with zoning incentives for permanent markets.
- Allow people in residential zones to grow and sell unprocessed produce on their property.
- Implement urban agriculture as an accessory use through the Living Building pilot program.
- Increase the number of chickens allowed from three to eight per dwelling unit.
- Allow miniature goats as small animals permitted in all zones as an accessory use with certain provisions.

As a result of these policies, commercial urban farms can be up to 10,000 square feet in neighborhood commercial zones (and much larger in other zones), gardens are allowed on rooftops, and residents can completely fill their yards with edible plants. Even more unusual is that residents can keep up to eight laying hens, and in lots over 10,000 square feet, they can keep cows, goats, sheep, and other farm animals. Unlike some cities, where food policies just seem designed to placate citizens, Seattle's changes are holistic and sincere.

This is in sharp contrast to many, many other city codes. For example, in the small town of Parksville, British Columbia, where I ended up borrowing the land to start a farm, the city made a big deal out of its new food policy allowing urban food gardens. The city now graciously allows you to use up to 20 percent of your yard for edible plants, and you may not sell your produce directly to the public. If you have a lot that's 10,000 square feet, minus the average 2,000 square feet of the house, that leaves you with 8,000 square feet of lawn, driveway, walkways and a few trees. You are then legally allowed to use up to 1,600 square feet of that for the garden. The remaining 6,400 square feet must be properly landscaped, mowed, and manicured. Just 2,500 square feet can feed four people all the produce they can eat for a year. Why limit it to 1,600?

In Seattle, the embrace of urban agriculture has been successful and transformative. According to reports prepared in 2011 by University of Washington urban design graduate students in partnership with the Regional Food Policy Council, Seattle now has at least seventy-five community gardens (and more planned). The smallest one is only 1,000 square feet, and the largest is Thistle Garden at 152,000 square feet, which serves 150 families. Altogether these gardens add up to 23 acres and feed 4,400 families, but demand is so high that twenty-nine have a waiting list of two years or more. There are also now at least ten successful farm businesses in the middle of the city, offering CSAs and selling at the markets.

One of the most important of these projects is the Beacon Hill Food Forest. Imagined by a team of four permaculture students, the food forest project was designed to be a seven-acre permanent, sustainable, edible forest in the middle of the city. These students studied through a partnership with Seattle Tilth, and as they told people about their final graduating project they began to gather tremendous support for realizing the idea. Soon they were joined by the Jefferson Park Alliance, and a new organization was born: the Friends of Beacon Food Forest. They received grants from the city for further development and planning, and in December 2011 won a grant of $100,000 to actually get things started. Seattle Public Utilities gave permission for the food forest to be placed adjacent to Jefferson Park. Hundreds of fruit trees were planted by a team of volunteers in the fall of 2012, with the hope that one day people would be able to walk through the city forest and pick pears and peaches during an afternoon stroll. Community support has made this project possible.

CHAPTER SIX

The Right to Eat

"And he gave it for his opinion, that whoever could make two ears of corn, or two blades of grass, to grow upon a spot of ground where only one grew before, would deserve better of mankind, and do more essential service to his country, than the whole race of politicians put together."

—Jonathan Swift, *Gulliver's Travels*

Defining Food Sovereignty

"Somewhere between 50 to 60 percent of the food you eat has been touched by immigrant hands, and it is fair to say some of them are not here as they should be here. But if you didn't have these folks, you would be spending a lot more—three, four, or five times more—for food, or we would have to import food and have all the food security risks."

—Tom Vilsack, head of the USDA

Tom Vilsack is correct that food would be five times more expensive without immigrant hands. He also says that if we import more food, we will be taking more food security risks. But what does that mean exactly?

Food security is access to safe, healthy food. This is usually only talked about on a household level, such as a family's ability to get to a full grocery store, or the affordability of vegetables. It is only at G-20 summits that we hear about discussions of food security on a global scale, and whether that food supply is safe and healthy. Vilsack is saying that if we import more food, we take a risk that our food is not as safe, and possibly not as reliable as it should be.

Greg Page, Chairman of Cargill, said at the 2012 Rio+20 summit, that

> Trade makes consumers less vulnerable to local shortages and the higher prices caused by bad weather, disease or civil disorder. Free trade helps feed a hungry world. Export restrictions and trading bans isolate local markets and give farmers little incentive to expand production for the next season. Governments must encourage open trade and a fair, transparent, rules-based system to everyone's gain, including the environment. And companies that are directly or indirectly in the business of feeding the world have a responsibility to promote trust-based free trade.

Cargill is the largest privately owned company in the United States, and its principal businesses are trading grain, animal feeds, and other food commodities.

Page's view is quite different than Vilsack's in terms of increasing food security, but it's in agreement with the common view of economists and policy developers. Is the ability to export and import *more* food the solution to our safety, affordability, and supply concerns?

Here's what Joel Salatin has to say in his book *Folks, This Ain't Normal: A Farmer's Advice for Happier Hens, Healthier People, and a Better World*:

> Food security is not in the supermarket. It's not in the government. It's not at the emergency services division. True food security is the historical normalcy of packing it in during the abundant times, building that in-house larder, and resting easy knowing that our little ones are not dependent on next week's farmers' market or the electronic cashiers at the supermarket.

Between Vilsack, Page, and Salatin, we have three opposing solutions to food security.

- We could build more large farms in our own country that rely on migrant workers.
- We could open up more international trade.
- Or we could grow food and preserve it for the winter.

Sometimes we confuse food security with food sovereignty. Food sovereignty is a phrase that was coined by Via Campesina, and defined as

> the right of peoples, communities, and countries to define their own agricultural, labour, fishing, food and land policies which are ecologically, socially, economically and culturally appropriate to their unique circumstances. It includes the true right to food and to produce food, which means that all people have the right to safe, nutritious and culturally appropriate food and to food-producing resources and the ability to sustain themselves and their societies. Food sovereignty means the primacy of people's and community's rights to food and food production, over trade concerns.

Food security, on the other hand, was defined in 1996 at the World Food Summit by the Food and Agriculture Organization of the United Nations as "when all people, at all times, have physical and economic access to sufficient, safe and nutritious food that meets their dietary needs and food preferences for an active and healthy life."

So, to sum up:

Food sovereignty = the right to have control over your food supply

Food security = the ability to access food

According to economists and critics of local food, food sovereignty is at odds with food security; if a country were to rely more on its own food production and give more control to individuals, food prices would increase and it would become more difficult to feed the growing population.

FOOD TYRANTS

In a country that is food sovereign, is the price of food more expensive, and is it more difficult to feed the masses? In France, as discussed earlier, food isn't really that expensive. However, this may be largely due to the subsidy system, which is keeping farmers paid and in business. At the same time, G-20 leaders (as they do in France) act with the responsibility of making third world countries more food secure, as well. These countries have policies in place to help Sub-Saharan Africa, and the number one mandate is to help small farmers. Small farmers in Africa face greater dangers than farmers in other countries because they are subject to extremes in weather, but they have no backup system to carry them through. Failure simply means starvation and death.

The G-20 countries, which include Canada, the United States, Mexico, Brazil, China, Japan, India, Russia, Germany, Italy, the United Kingdom, France, and Australia, represent 65 percent of the world's farmland and 77 percent of the world's grain output. At the same time, food production will have to increase 70 percent by 2050 to keep up with the growing population, and unless it does, our global food security will decrease. When Canada and Australia's grain crop failed in 2008 because of drought and floods, a phenomenon that is predicted to become more frequent, prices went up. An increase in prices limits the affordability for some countries that don't grow enough and depend on those grain crops. When too many food crops fail and people can't afford the increased prices, they riot. It doesn't really take much for this to happen when you consider that people in urban areas of India and China have to spend half of their income for the same amount of food we spend about 10 percent of our income for. A month or two of higher food prices can make them vulnerable and even homeless.

Unfortunately, increasing food production is very difficult, not only because of the loss of farmland and farmers, but also because for every one degree the world heats up due to climate change, we lose 10 percent of our global food production. The G-20 leaders are trying to get everyone to work together now to try to buy some insurance for the future. Some are trying to gain more food security with greater food sovereignty and some are not.

No Time for Apathy

"Imagine all the food mankind has produced over the past 8,000 years. Now consider that we need to produce that same amount again—but in just the next forty years if we are to feed our growing and hungry world."
—Paul Polman, CEO of Unilever and Daniel Servitje,
CEO of Group Bimbo

By 2050, 9 billion people will inhabit the earth. Almost a billion people do not have enough food right now. Our water supply is decreasing rapidly. It is even more disastrous knowing that 40 percent of the crops we produce are wasted, due to transportation, restaurants, and the need for perfect-looking vegetables. Since we use 70 percent of the available fresh water for agriculture, it is estimated that a quarter of our water supply is used for wasted food. Fossil fuels are wasted in the process as well, totaling an estimated 300 million barrels of oil per year, or 4 percent of the US consumption (Hall).

On top of this, Americans are getting ever more obese. Scientists think that one reason this is happening is because there is too much food available to them. Like animals in the wild, humans have developed a tendency to eat when there is food available in order to store up fat for later. Feast or famine is in our biology. Meanwhile in places like Africa and India, which just can't produce enough food for their population, it's going to get tougher as we move forward. This is why CEOs and world leaders are pushing for easier trade across countries' borders; there shouldn't be waste and obesity in one country while another goes hungry.

However, this argument fails to address the real source of the problem. Americans (and Canadians) have too much food, but it's also the wrong kinds of food. We are using grain to feed cows and overproducing corn for biofuels and corn syrup. We could feed at least 800 million people with the grain that we hand over to the feedlot cattle that are not very good at converting energy to protein. In fact, the cattle output ratio of energy to protein is 54:1 versus a broiler chicken's 4:1. More than half of our grain production is being fed to 8 billion livestock, and every pound of beef requires 11,973 gallons of water to produce it, not because the cow is that thirsty, but because of all the grain it takes to feed it. Ninety percent of the soil is eroding at thirteen times the sustainable rate because of cattle farming. If animals are raised on pasture, this kind of waste can be eliminated.

The average adult male needs about 56 grams of protein per day, but America produces enough for every man, woman, and child to have 75 grams of protein per day. Even if all the grain used for livestock production were exported and the cattle switched over to pasture, Americans would still have 29 grams of animal protein per day. Fortunately, the United States already produces enough plant protein to make up the difference. This change in diet would be enough to decrease obesity, prevent soil erosion, and help the economy (Cornell).

So what's going to happen if we stay on our present course? It's not a very pleasant picture. In the next forty years, we'll see farmers having more and more difficulty producing the same crops. More grain farmers will lose a year's production due to flooding and drought due to poor soil management, and as temperatures and moisture levels change so will the myriad plant diseases and fungi that attack crops. Because of this, many farmers will turn to greater quantities of pesticides and fungicides, and politicians will feel pressured to approve more GM crops. At the same time, food prices will go up as commodity supplies dwindle. Sometimes these skyrocketing prices will make sense because something will actually be more scarce, but sometimes stores will just make the prices higher due to volatility. These food prices will eventually be comparable to those in Europe and Japan.

There is an opportunity here that needs to be recognized. While small, local farmers will face the same struggles with weather that everyone else will, their prices will no longer be higher than anyone else's. Small farmers who sell direct to consumers tend to have more stable prices because they do not fall victim to the supply chain that reacts to the whims of the economy or global trade. People will begin to realize this and local food won't be something only affluent people seek out.

Meanwhile farmers are retiring. The old system will inevitably begin to change as a new generation of farmers replaces the last. Young people who get into farming have an opportunity to find news ways to farm and distribute food. Part of this is changing what we eat, what we grow, and where we grow it.

Even though the opportunity exists, we are facing a seemingly insurmountable struggle. Food prices will rise drastically, but most likely only for the crops we are used to eating, like corn, wheat, beef, apples, and other staple foods. This is partially because of oil prices creeping higher and higher. Industrial agriculture is heavily reliant on petroleum, through the use of machinery, transportation, and oil-produced fertilizer and pesticides. We aren't supposed to have any kind of oil supply problem, and yet oil prices have more than doubled in the last decade. This is due to political climates in the Middle East, violent storms that destroy offshore refineries, and the supply-and-demand ratio that hasn't been effectively controlled by the Organization of the Petroleum Exporting Countries (OPEC). Even if supply was going to be a problem, it is doubtful that any oil company would admit it.

This scenario of cumulative forces is going to make us all uncomfortable. Even the wealthiest people will feel it because they may notice they're the only ones who can continue eating what they've always eaten. Water and land are in short supply, the population is exploding, the climate is changing, and it's all happening so quickly. Oxfam, the international charity that works to alleviate poverty, estimates that food prices will be double what they are today by 2030. That's only eighteen years from now. Today the average North American family of four spends between $1,000 and $1,300 per month on food, according to the USDA, but by 2030 they will be spending $2,000 to $2,600. There is no way the average middle class family will be able to manage this, especially if the economy does not improve.

There's no time to argue whether this is going to happen. We can talk about sustainability for the earth and healthy food all day long, but it may very well just come down to cost. Will you be able to afford the same foods you were eating before? Probably not, and they probably won't even be available in the same quantities. You will have to grow some of your food yourself, even just to be able to have some fresh vegetables.

The solution to most of these problems lies in local control of the food supply. Not only will you have to grow some of your food to afford what you eat, there will need to be a local movement to facilitate food distribution at a regional level as well. While there are many optimistic people who would rather rely on trade and genetic modification to solve these puzzles, they are just bandages for a bigger problem. We have to decide which kind of insecurity to pick. Do we choose to trust the global market and put our food in the hands of a few corporations who ship food all over the world? Or do we choose local production, which is more subject to crop failure due to weather? Frankly, I would rather choose the latter because it is in my own hands. I have lost trust in the global system and the corporations.

This means growing certain foods that grow well where you live. For example, spinach is a high-value crop where I live, but it takes a lot of water to grow and it doesn't tolerate heat very well. In midsummer it immediately goes to seed. A good alternative is New Zealand spinach, which isn't a true spinach at all, but it tastes like it. (In fact, I like the taste better.) It tolerates heat and drought and has a high nutritional value. The only reason this valuable vegetable isn't found at stores is because it can't be harvested with machines the same way. Finding species like this and growing them locally is the solution to our food crises.

The Right to Food

"For now I ask no more,
Than the justice of eating."

—Pablo Neruda, Chilean Poet, Nobel Prize Winner

One of the fundamental stumbling blocks limiting humanity's progress in feeding all its members is our terrible habit of questioning whether food is a right. It is as though we (and by *we*, I mean developed nations) still have a primitive mindset that if the weaker people die, it's their own fault for being weak. Perhaps from a harsh evolutionary standpoint some think that mass starvation due to overpopulation is just the earth reclaiming balance. They ignore the fact that such reclamation would only pick off the poorest people, leaving only the wealthiest.

Right now there's really no excuse, though, because we produce enough to feed everyone but we don't give it to them. We also produce foods that have no real value when we could be growing better ones. The Food and Agriculture Organization of the UN has determined that people are only hungry in the world because of poverty, not supply, because food prices are overinflated due to far-reaching policies and trade. The United States put 23 percent of its grain production into making ethanol in 2007, but this only made up 4.5 percent of the fuel sales (Eide). Globally, agrofuels make up 1 percent of the world's fuel, but use a ridiculous amount of grain production to make them. In 2010, a USDA analysis found that the grain used to make fuel had increased to 25 percent and farmers were pushing for even greater production because of the government's mandate in 2007 that the United States increase ethanol production 500 percent by 2017. Meanwhile this misguided "ecological" direction has been one of the major factors that increased food prices 75 percent between 2002 and 2008 according to a report by the World Bank (Mitchell). This secret report was not meant for the public's eye, but was accidentally discovered by the *Guardian* and published. It means that while we have all of these other factors helping to increase food prices, the major cause is biofuels. This report was prepared because food prices had suddenly increased 74 percent in one year (2006) and 20 percent in the previous three months. These prices did go down eventually, but in 2012 they were right back up there again. The averages continue to rise, but this would be preventable on a grade scale if the priority wasn't profits from an inefficient fuel source.

While it would be nice to trust the global system and policy, it's just not very reliable. Over and over again it has been demonstrated that food-related corporations care about profits over the well-being of humanity. Even though the cause of rising food prices due to ethanol production was recognized as far back as 2007, there has been almost no change in the way we do things, and food prices are still rising. This is a fundamental attack on everyone's right to food. Meanwhile, we are still debating whether food is a right and how much we should do to fulfill that right.

Jean Zeigler, the UN Special Rapporteur on the Right to Food, concluded that the right to food entails "the right to have regular, permanent and unrestricted access, either directly or by means of financial purchases, to quantitatively and qualitatively adequate and sufficient food corresponding to the cultural traditions of the people to which the consumer belongs, and which ensures a physical and mental, individual and collective, fulfilling and dignified life free of fear."

Food policy in North America fails severely on all of these levels. City bylaws restrict direct access to homegrown food, food prices are becoming prohibitively high, many people cannot access the foods that their culture eats (because we are a multicultural society after all), and a huge number of people live in fear that they will not be able to feed themselves or their children. In 2012, Zeigler investigated Canada as the FAO's Right to Food envoy and found that 800,000 people (or 7 percent) were too poor to eat well. He slammed Canada's inequality and hypocrisy, saying, "It's not because the country is a wealthy country that there are no problems. In fact, the problems are very significant and, frankly, this sort of self-righteousness about the situation being good in Canada is not corresponding to what I saw on the ground, not at all" (Schmidt). Meanwhile in the United States, 14 percent of households are food insecure, which equals about 17 million households (Coleman-Jensen).

Is food a right? Is water a right? Is shelter a right? Is safety from violence and crime a right? According to the Canadian government it is, illustrated by the signing of the United Nations International Covenant on Economic, Social and Cultural Rights. In fact, the only countries in the world that have not recognized the right to food through some legal means or UN covenant are Greenland, Puerto Rico, Western Sahara, Southern Sudan, Botswana, Burma, Bhutan, Malaysia (give or take a few islands), and . . . the United States.

Navigating food policy and predicting the future is a daunting and exhausting task. Obviously things aren't going so well, and we can talk about building a culture of sustainable food, but if the general attitude is that food is a privilege rather than a right, there will be no change towards a positive solution. One point that has been made by critics repeatedly is that local, organic food is only for the affluent. This is unfortunately true: 15 percent of people who buy organic are more well-off than the rest of the population, and they are buying 5 percent of the produce. These people have been accused of being elitist, and small farmers have been accused of catering to their spoiled and specialized taste buds. There doesn't seem to be a clear picture for the future, or a sustainable model that will work for everyone.

If food is a right, then these choices must be made available and affordable to everyone regardless of income.

City Farms as the Roadmap to Change

"You never change things by fighting the existing reality. To change something, build a new model that makes the existing model obsolete."

—Richard Buckminster

There are two ways a farm can be successful, and success requires a reliable income. Rural farms are far away from the urban or suburban consumer, and thus rely on a distribution system to get food to the buyer. In Canada, 80 percent of the population lives in an urban area, in the United States it's 82 percent, and in the United Kingdom it's 90 percent. These numbers are only going to grow in the future (Brown). However, most "city dwellers" actually have backyards, however small. We know that 2,500 square feet can provide a family of four with all the produce they need with backyard chickens and beans providing the protein.

One of the best examples of an urban produce farm is Growing Power, located in Milwaukee, Wisconsin. Started by the charismatic (and now famous) Will Allen, Growing Power produces a million pounds of food on his original three-acre city lot. He pioneered aquaculture and greenhouse techniques now mirrored by thousands of farmers, which earned him a spot on *Time* magazine's list of the most influential people of 2010. If the average person eats 1.5 pounds of fruit and vegetables a day and a half a pound of meat, that's 712 pounds of vegetables and protein a year. This means that Allen's three acres produce enough vegetables and protein for 1,329 people.

Metro Milwaukee has a population of 1.5 million people. Is it feasible or even possible for small farms like Growing Power to meet the produce and protein needs of Milwaukee? Suppose a quarter of the population had a backyard garden, and produced half of what they needed. That frees up enough food for 166 more people, which means that 1,495 people can get their fruit, vegetables, and protein from a three-acre farm and some backyards. To feed the city of Milwaukee, there would need to be 1,003 similar farms covering 3,009 acres.

Then there is grain. Most of us think that grain must be grown on thousands of acres using massive machines, but it is possible to grow it on a small scale. Projects like Lawns to Loaves in Vancouver, British Columbia, are trying to demonstrate that grain can be grown in the city. In their first year twenty-five people planted 100 square feet of wheat each, or 2,500 square feet and harvested fifty pounds of wheat. This is on the low end of wheat yield. On the high end this same area could produce 125 pounds of wheat or 325 pounds of rice. The average person eats half a pound of grain per day, or 132 pounds per year. With the right kinds of grains, that magical number of 2,500 square feet can feed a person all the grain needed in a year or seventeen people per acre. This means that it takes 86,000 acres to grow the grain for the city of Milwaukee.

This seems like a tremendous amount of land. Add the 3,000 acres used to grow vegetables and protein to the 86,000 acres and it would take 89,000 acres to feed everyone in Milwaukee. This seems like it would be impossible in an urban area, despite efforts like Growing Power. The city of Milwaukee covers 97 square miles, or 62,000 acres. If as much of this land as possible was used for agriculture, in the form of abandoned lots, backyard farms, rooftop farms, and indoor farms (like Sweet Water Organics, which grows vertically under lights in a reclaimed warehouse), the rest could be covered by a green belt outside the city. Milwaukee County currently has farms covering 5,458 acres, but according to Wisconsin Public Policy Forum, the county has 38,833 acres of available land. Thus we find that the most urbanized county in Wisconsin still has half of the rural acreage it needs to feed its population, and a majority share of the other half could be made up of urban land.

The 100-mile diet is still just the right radius for food sovereignty, even in this very urban county. At its widest point, Milwaukee County is fifty miles wide, and while the city of Milwaukee probably would not be able to feed itself within its borders, on a countywide basis it could.

It is true that it is less efficient to grow vegetables in Milwaukee than it is in Mexico. The growing conditions are not ideal for our most popular vegetables and fruit, but we can't grow everything in California and Arizona because that's just not sustainable. We don't have enough water to do that. It's a difficult decision to choose inefficiency over profits. Many "experts" claim that the solution is to trust our corporate leaders, but who stands to win from that scenario? Only one group will profit from that solution, and it's the food tyrants who helped to create this system in the first place. In these troubled economic times, the only thing that will pull us out of this food crisis is the same thing that will help pull us out of the recession. By putting money into localizing farms, billions of dollars of otherwise corporate money will stay within our local economies. Food is a big business, to the tune of more than $184 *billion* dollars every year in the United States Most of this goes into the pockets of companies in the distribution system. What would happen if this money stayed at home?

There are some who argue that commercial development on valuable land is what helps economies. They want developers to purchase open land, develop it, and sell houses and lease buildings to businesses. However, this is a top-down strategy. Food is the ultimate bottom-up strategy. It is an industry that employs untrained people and youth who would otherwise have a difficult time finding employment. It is reliable in that there's always a market for it (if it's not a commodity crop), and when consumers pay the farmer directly, that farmer will then purchase materials and equipment locally. For example, when our farm needed a large quantity of lumber and plastic, we were paid directly by the consumer for a CSA share. That money went straight to a locally owned hardware store that pays several employees, plus we paid a couple of farm workers who helped build the beds. These employees purchase their items locally, including food and services, and the cycle continues. Every dollar spent locally creates 45 to 65 percent of value within the community. This is called the *local multiplier effect,* and it means that every $100 spent in a town creates $45 more.

In the current system, money spent on food at the grocery store goes through the distribution system and finally funnels into the pockets of a company far away. Eighty percent of the money you spend leaves the community, never to be seen again. This is because the people who made the product aren't local, the goods aren't local, and the only one who sees any of it is the grocery store and the corporation that brought it in. Every $100 spent at a chain or big box store only creates $14 for the community, which is really a loss of $31 compared to a local purchase. In urbanized Milwaukee County alone, agriculture is currently a $6 billion industry. If this agricultural product is being shipped out rather than sold locally, the county economy is losing almost $2 billion dollars per year. That's $2,000 for every man, woman and child in Milwaukee County.

To anyone who doubts that urban space can produce even a fraction of the food a city needs, one need only to look at Havana, Cuba. Two hundred gardens throughout the city produce an amazing 90 percent of the residents' food from an estimated 85,000 acres of land. With a population of more than 2 million, this is no small feat. The rest of Cuba is also a shining example of food sovereignty and produces 70 percent of its own food. This began in the 1980s when the Cuban government recognized that the country would soon be facing an insurmountable economic crisis. Dependent on only a few crops and help from the USSR, agriculture experts immediately began mobilizing small-scale agriculture all over the country. They changed from a large-scale monoculture export system to a small-scale, self-sufficient urban system within a decade. Although the economic troubles of the 1990s were far more overwhelming than the Cuban government had even foreseen, the urban agriculture they had in place helped tremendously, and they focused their efforts on intensifying this strategy, with great success. It makes sense because 80 percent of

Cuba's population is urban as well. They created farmland by using raised beds, ripping up parking lots, and encouraging citizens to use all their yard space for growing food. The specific goal they were working toward was to provide every fifteen houses with a growing space, and they achieved this goal. The Ministry of Agriculture has also placed knowledge and organic growing supplies within easy access, employing a mind-boggling sixty-seven agriculture extension agents by 1997. They experimented on a wide scale with the System of Rice Intensification, which they proved could at least double rice yields. In effect, the Ministry of Agriculture made everyone a farmer. Twenty-two percent of all the new jobs created after the economic crisis have been in agriculture, and food security has risen. Before the crisis, 6 percent of Cuba's population was food insecure, and that rose to 18 percent during the crisis. Today, Cuba is back down to 6 percent (FAO).

The 5,000-square-foot estimate (2,500 of vegetables and 2,500 of grains) needed to feed each person is feasible but depends on new intensive growing techniques like square-foot gardening, raised beds, aquaculture, and plastic tunnels. This number is actually incredibly small when compared to the space it currently takes to feed you, which is about 48,437 square feet. Shrinking this space down to 5,000 square feet takes a great deal of effort to build up optimum growing conditions. It means fixing nonideal soil with massive amounts of compost, removing rocks, building raised beds, creating microclimates with indoor growing spaces, and carefully reclaiming wastewater. This kind of change takes more involvement by more people. It means switching from a system that relies on machinery and large spaces to one that relies on more people and small spaces. It doesn't mean abandoning technology or going back to the dark ages. It means embracing new, sustainable technologies that already exist (like aquaculture) to help create less labor and less risk in a perilous world on the brink of massive change.

Starting an Urban Farm, Co-op or CSA

"There seem to be but three ways for a nation to acquire wealth. The first is by war, as the Romans did, in plundering their conquered neighbors. This is robbery. The second is by commerce, which is generally cheating. The third is by agriculture, the only honest way, wherein man receives a real increase of the seed thrown into the ground, in a kind of continual miracle, wrought by the hand of God in his favor, as a reward for his innocent life and his virtuous industry."

—Benjamin Franklin

Mark Twain once said, "There is no sadder sight than a young pessimist, except an old optimist." Farmers are often accused of being continual optimists, or even chronic gamblers. The process of farming does feel like gambling sometimes. You plant the seeds and do everything you can and *hope* for a good crop. There is never certainty. However, this is the way that humanity has survived for thousands of years, and no matter how hard we try to avoid it, we will continue to have to farm for thousands more. In these modern times, there's no excuse for not having more control of your food. While the previous sections talked about home gardening and saving seed, this section addresses the serious need for more farmers, or those who will grow food at least part time on a serious basis on a larger scale. You don't need be a farmer, however. There are three good ways to get involved, and two of them don't necessarily mean growing food (although they could): the co-op, CSA, and urban farm.

The Co-op

A cooperative (or co-op) is a collaboration between like-minded individuals who are working towards a common goal. They are increasingly recognized for their ability to make good things happen, so much so that the United Nations partnered with the International Cooperative Alliance to declare

2012 the International Year of Cooperatives. Cooperative enterprises work differently from other businesses in that they are based on needs and values rather than profits. There are many different forms of cooperatives, but we are most interested for the purposes of this book in agriculture and food co-ops. Cooperatives aren't just little groups run by Birkenstock-wearing health nuts. Companies like Ocean Spray, Ace Hardware, Sunkist, and the Associated Press are all cooperatives.

Anyone can start a co-op, and it is one of the best and easiest ways to get more hands-on with locally grown food while supporting local farms. The farmers' market is often inconvenient, and most families with children have difficulty acquiring all their food there. The co-op makes it possible to bring in food more conveniently from farms that may be slightly farther away. Since urban farms can't grow all the food, the 100-mile area has to be included, but it is not efficient or feasible for everyone to drive 100 miles to get food. By pooling resources, co-op members can designate one person to be in charge of acquiring food, and with a larger financial purse, the co-op can have bulk buying power to get food cheaper.

Food co-ops work on a few basic principles. Membership is open to anyone who agrees with the cooperative principles and is not limited by any religious or social beliefs. The members own the co-op, and as owners they have to put up the money needed to run it. In return each member has equal say and gets one vote in all decision making. Co-ops are independent and are not influenced by any outside businesses or agencies, although they may help out other cooperatives. The ICA has issued this statement on the cooperative identity: "Cooperatives are based on the values of self-help, self-responsibility, democracy, equality, equity, and solidarity. In the tradition of their founders, cooperative members believe in the ethical values of honesty, openness, social responsibility, and caring for others."

A co-op has a board of directors, who oversee the cooperative on behalf of the members. This board acts as trustees by taking responsibility for the financial side, maintaining responsible accounting, publishing timely reports, and making sure all appropriate laws are followed. They hire the manager, if there is a paid business manager, and they make long-term goals for the co-op. Good co-op boards aren't micromanagers, however. While they hire the managers and are held accountable for the management's actions, the management actually runs the day-to-day operation. The board usually meets monthly and has training on a regular basis to help directors do their jobs better.

The money needed for a food co-op comes from its members. This means each member pays a membership fee, usually yearly. They may also ask for a microloan that gets paid back when the member leaves, such as Karma Co-op in Toronto that requests $100. They may ask for a couple of volunteer hours per month in exchange for waiving some fees or for lower prices. Every co-op is different, but most ask for a $150 to $200 investment on top of the food cost. Some are quite big and operate out of a retail store that offers many services, such as catering and natural products at Outpost Coop in Milwaukee. Some are quite small and operate out of a garage.

The garage co-op is possibly the most important cooperative. The simple act of getting people together at someone's house for a greater cause has the power to make tremendous change. In the incredibly personal and important documentary *The Real Dirt on Farmer John*, John Peterson shares his personal struggle with farm life and the ever-present battle over finances. It wasn't until city dwellers approached him with a bulk-buying offer that things turned around for him. These brave souls originally helped distribute food out of a garage, and Angelic Organics is now one of the largest CSAs in the United States. There are many food cooperatives that involve a group of moms who pool some money so that they can purchase bulk amounts of dry beans and whole wheat from wholesale catalogs, but that isn't much different than a grocery store. Food co-ops need to take an inventory of all the farms in the greater area, that 100-mile or county region, and have someone who keeps track of what each one has available. With the bulk purchasing power of a pooled bank account, co-ops can buy large quantities straight from farmers.

You might think that farmers wouldn't want the hassle of having to deal with a co-op, but the opposite is true. Farmers struggle to find large, reliable buyers. They arm wrestle with restaurant owners, who offer to buy large amounts on a weekly basis but tend to be quite picky. Having a buyer who purchases large amounts regularly provides financial stability. This is a massive benefit to farmers who now don't have to rely solely on the farmers' market, can make just one delivery, and don't need as much less labor. The co-op is the perfect solution because there is no middleman between the sacred farmer-customer relationship, and yet there is more security. The co-op members are able to buy food more conveniently from many farms at lower prices, and the farmer is able to run a reliable business that requires less labor.

Starting a co-op with a bunch of friends is quite easy, but to really get the purchasing power you need and make it a good deal for the farmers, having at least 100 members is ideal. If each member puts in $40 per week for a box of food, that gives the co-op $4,000 each week. This money can go towards fruit, vegetables, grains, meats, eggs, and dairy in decent quantities. The more members, the more food each member will get. It is important that the manager and assistants have a clear understanding of the types of things the members want in their box, and hopefully some expertise in local food and its value. Negotiating with farmers could be frustrating if the co-op manager has no idea what the regional price structure is or has difficulty developing relationships with farmers. For example, in my area, organic strawberries in season sell for about $10 per pound retail, but $3 per pound wholesale. The food co-op can offer the farmer a better deal, by paying higher than wholesale and saving him labor, but still save money on the retail price. For a co-op to operate well, the following must occur:

- It is important that the financial side be kept simple and separate. The co-op should have its own bank account, and someone needs to be in charge of weekly accounting. A monthly statement needs to be issued to all members.
- Someone needs to be in charge of getting the food and then distributing it to the members in a timely manner. Food is time sensitive when it's not being refrigerated. Produce can last a little while, but meat and dairy need almost constant refrigeration. Members need to pick up their deliveries quickly, or the garage needs to have a couple of refrigerators to handle those items.
- Transporting some items over long distances means the necessity of having coolers with ice. The larger the co-op, the more likely it is that there could be a refrigerated truck, professional cooler, and a full-time staff person.
- Even without this paid employee, a food co-op needs to have at least four dedicated volunteers who each have responsibility over a specific job. These individuals will quickly gain an appreciation for how much work it takes to distribute food, and hopefully they would be provided with some form of payment, even if it is extra food.

The step up from a food co-op is a farmers' or agricultural co-op. The agricultural cooperative has many of the same benefits as a food co-op, including the paramount one of shared risk. A farm co-op has shared ownership and a larger labor pool that produces more crops. When production increases and is pooled together, it does two things: It ensures that there is always a good crop, and it lowers the costs of production. Farmers' co-ops can either be formed of several privately owned farms, or something increasingly common, a farm owned cooperatively. (As mentioned earlier that the majority of French farms now follow this model.) Forming a farm this way is the most viable way for young people to acquire large acreage and become financially successful without too much individual burden of debt. What it is not is a commune. It's strictly a business arrangement. Historically, these farms do not benefit the poorest people in the co-op because it takes a significant financial investment to start a good farm, but once the strongest members begin it, opportunity exists to allow others in with smaller investment.

Farmers' co-ops follow the same principles as any other cooperative, but for young people wanting to buy a farm, they usually mean living together on the same property. This means that membership cannot be so open and there may be restrictions on some personal beliefs or lifestyle choices. For the sake of the longevity of the co-op, each member must have separate living quarters, even in the beginning. The farm is a business arrangement, and it is important to keep personal affairs and business separate. These lines become blurred when you share a kitchen. It is also important that each farmer-member have the ability to have his or her own land space and crops. Farmers' co-ops often have a slightly different voting strategy based on production. Because some farmers produce more crops than others, they carry more of the risk and therefore deserve a more powerful vote. Votes may be added based on tons of food or the economic value of crops.

There can't be any outside investment when starting a farm cooperative for the purchase of land or for selling crops. This is one of the basic principles of co-ops, because it creates a conflict of interest. Rather than focusing on building infrastructure or growing crops, the secondary goal of an interested third party can be distracting or worse, destructive. To start a farmers' co-op, the first investment goal is for acquiring and developing land. This may be urban land, either borrowed or leased, or rural land, which can be bought or leased. I won't even talk about buying urban land, which is hardly ever feasible. Whether the land is free or not, money must be available to build the land up for farming, in the form of inputs (compost and seeds), raised beds, high tunnels, irrigation, and fencing. This part of the investment should be pooled, with that same amount saved in a fund that can buy out farmers who choose to leave the cooperative. In this situation, the land would not be owned by any one person, but rather owned by the co-op, and members would own shares based on their investment.

For those interested in this kind of serious involvement in farming, a few key pieces of information are needed. This knowledge is not always freely available and yet is extremely important for young people to know when getting into agriculture:

- A project in a rural area requires an investment of at least $200,000, depending on the price of the land and what kind of infrastructure is on it. At least $60,000 of that has to go to developing the growing area, inputs, and tools. A half-acre space with a couple of homemade high tunnels costs at least $15,000 to prepare for intensive growing, and for a co-op, two acres is the minimum for a profitable enterprise. It may be possible to find some land for $140,000, but keep in mind that it must be within the 100-mile radius of a city, and preferably at the most within 45 miles. That's the maximum driving time for delivering produce, so the closer to your market the better.

- A project in an urban area using borrowed land (such as SPIN farming, or Small Plot INtensive farming) requires an investment of at least $30,000. This is used to purchase inputs, a rototiller, refrigeration equipment, a truck, and other tools. These can be shared among several urban farmers operating out of backyards or leased land. The profits per square foot are higher in the city because the initial investment is so much lower and the market price is higher, but these farms tend to be smaller. The smaller the farm, the less likely the farmer can do it without a second job to support it. An equipment (and labor) co-op can make it possible for urban farms to do things on a larger scale. For example, many use old refrigerators, but a professional walk-in cooler can hold an entire crop. This is so important when harvesting for a Saturday farmers' market that opens at 8 a.m., because everything needs to be harvested on Friday.

A second kind of farmer cooperative manages only product marketing for a group of farmers. Many established farms today are members of a cooperative, which they formed to purchase their own product. The co-op, as a separate entity, purchases the crops of all the farmers and then handles the selling and/or distribution. Usually that means handling negotiations with a wholesaler, but today a co-op can become a direct selling machine, whether in the form of a CSA or a physical market. The labor involved in distributing farm product is taken from the farmers so they can spend more time growing, and there is much less risk because if one farmer has a shortfall, the other farms can fill it. The cooperative can also purchase expensive equipment, like the large coolers and refrigerated trucks that a single farm might not be able to afford. It is important to remember that although a marketing cooperative like this is for making money, the ultimate goal is not higher profits. In fact, profits might be a little lower for the farmer on a per item basis because he is selling at a lower-than-retail rate to the co-op. The benefits are in cost and labor savings, shared risk, and less stress.

Success as an agricultural co-op depends on a couple of important factors:

- Marketing co-ops need someone in charge with a strong marketing background. This means understanding branding, current internet selling techniques like social media, and the ability to keep track of current food events and policy.
- Distribution on a co-op level for farms is not the same as for a food co-op. A food co-op just has to get a fraction of the food to the customer in a timely manner. Coordinating the harvest of several entire farms, handling proper processing and storage for optimum freshness, and managing multiple types of customers takes a skilled person. Co-ops will usually have enough products to run a CSA, show up at the farmers' market, sell to restaurants, and possibly run a full-time farm stand. This manager will need several assistants.

The CSA

Don't start out financing your first farm equipment by creating a CSA. Community Supported Agriculture operates on the principle of shared risk, but customers expect you to have the risks worked out as much as possible. The customers agree to take a loss on their investment if things go wrong, and since they pay up front at the beginning of the season, there's nothing they can do about it. If you do operate a CSA in your first year, be prepared to refund people's money if things go wrong.

A CSA operating out of one farm (rather than a co-op) is a challenge because you have to grow so many varieties of food, and they have to be planted in succession so that crops are ready every week of the season. The knowledge and planning required to pull this off comes with time and is incredibly challenging in the first year. It is much better to plant a few high-profit crops, grow several varieties of those crops so you can pinpoint which ones do the best in your area and soil, and raise some animals on the side. Dairy, eggs, chickens, lambs, and goats are reliable moneymakers that can be managed without much more labor. These can be sold on the farm or at the farmers' market and are a good, relatively low-stress way to start.

That being said, the CSA is a phenomenal way of creating farm income where there otherwise wouldn't be any. Rather than waiting until July or August to make money, when the crops start coming in, a CSA brings in money in March. This means having cash to purchase inputs like seeds and fertilizer when you need it. In return, the farm promises to provide a share of the harvest to the members each week, at a fair market value. This usually averages around 4 to 10 pounds of food per week, since most CSAs charge around $30 to $40 per week. The beginning of the season features more salad greens and cold-weather crops, making the delivery lighter, but towards the end of the year it balances out with heavy crops like squash, potatoes, melons, and fruit. CSAs tend to cater to the more affluent customer who is looking for a more involved experience with the farm, because the up front cost is usually $300 to $900. These people don't mind picking up their share at the farm every week or will pay extra for delivery.

It's crucial not to reinvent the wheel with a CSA, especially in the beginning stages. The CSA model is now widely accepted and recognized by customers who are willing to bend over backwards to help a farm out, including volunteering, handling pickup points, and providing emergency donations. Farms don't have to try to one-up the competition with lower prices or even more services. Keep it simple. Competing on quality and dependability doesn't cost more, as opposed to other ways of competing; it just takes planning and effort.

Many studies have been done on CSAs, and what you can expect is somewhat predictable. This information has also been confirmed by own experience running a CSA:

- A traditionally farmed row-crop farm using mechanization can expect to produce 30 shares per acre. That doesn't mean that the acre is going to just feed 30 families; it means that as a general rule, planning for losses, no more than 30 units should be sold. An intensively planted farm can offer up to 50 shares per acre when well-established, but is unlikely to be able to farm more than 2 acres without a lot more labor.
- Intensive farming requires at least five people per half an acre to take care of the weeding and harvesting, and the more land, the more people it takes. At the two-acre level the farm should have fifteen to twenty people involved at various times of the year. A mechanized farm can use five people for five acres.
- The farm must plant at least 30 to 40 varieties, and each share is built around a large salad. In some areas a mixed baby green bag is expected (mesclun mix), and in others a large head of lettuce is the norm. Early in the season things like broccoli, kale, cabbage, and turnips fill in the weight, and later in the season the tomatoes, zucchini, cucumbers, and potatoes fill it in. Baby greens are a challenge because a new crop must be ready every week, and each crop can only be harvest during a

two-week period. This means planting every two weeks for harvesting 30 to 37 days later. CSA farms tend to carefully guard their planting schedule and variety list because of the tremendous amount of work it takes to develop it. However, this just slows progress. Eventually the other farmers will work it out, so why be secretive? It is much better to share seeds and varieties that work so that species and techniques can be improved.

- Once the maximum farm customers are obtained according to the space you have, the next step is *not* expansion to more land or trying to get more customers. It is more profitable to maximize production and create more value. Value-added products are ones that are processed from farm crops, such as jam, pickles, and tea. Not only can you make many of these items from *seconds*, that is, crops that are too ugly to sell, you can charge more than you could for the raw item. These can be sold as add-ons to your existing customers, along with eggs and meat, and can be sold at your farm stand. Meanwhile work hard to build up your soil and perfect your growing techniques for greater and more reliable yields.

- Distribution can be done by home delivery, delivery to drop-off points, and/or pick-up at the farm. Each has its merits and drawbacks. Home delivery puts distribution completely in the hands of the farm, but takes more labor. For the farmer all the customers should be within a 30-mile radius, otherwise it's not worth the fuel and time. It takes less time to do this than to allow farm pick-up, but you have to have a very good delivery database system on the computer that keeps track of the customers, the routes, and whether they will be around or not. Deliveries also have to be made in the evening when people are home. Delivery to drop-off points is a happy compromise but usually relies on an outside source to provide the location, such as a parking lot or even a member's garage. Many farms have a relationship with a member that allows them to drop off the food at a spot and leave, and allows shareholders to pick up when they can during a three-hour period. Pick-up at the farm works if the farm is close to the shareholders and has ample parking. The shares can be left out and people can serve themselves without too much trouble.

The Urban Farm

The final piece of the puzzle is the urban farm. Actually, more often than not, urban farms are really suburban farms, taking advantage of someone's under-used suburban hobby farm acreage. This land is either leased or borrowed. Leasing may not necessarily have any additional security as opposed to a verbal agreement for borrowed land, because the farmer is only leasing a section of the property. The property owner can still kick you off, but at the very least you might be able to get a deposit back or make sure you can retain any property that you have there, such as tools or a greenhouse. Without a paper agreement outlining this, the property owner can take everything you have built up there. Verbal agreements only work well if the person you're dealing with is trustworthy, but even then, having something in writing is a good idea.

Loss of farmland is the biggest complaint of urban farms, and this is why the farming techniques are slightly different. For borrowed or leased land that is not owned by a very trusted person, raised beds and permanent structures take too much time and money, unless there is absolute certainty that the property can be farmed for the next five years. In five years it will have paid for itself so it won't matter anymore. Otherwise the property must have existing soil, and a rototiller must be used. The farmer will be able to go in, quickly add inputs, and turn the soil and produce a crop right away without much investment.

Urban farms also cannot usually be certified organic because they do not have adequate buffers. Gardens growing on the edges of roads and highways have a higher lead content because of deposits in the soil, and this is why certified organic crops must have a buffer zone, either of a certain amount of space or a tree belt to absorb the exhaust fumes. To combat this, urban farmers must add even more compost to the soil. The more organic material, the less concentrated the lead and other toxins will be. Mulches can also help.

One major benefit of urban farming is the close proximity to customers. Some even have farm stands set up right on the sidewalk like lemonade stands. Most cities have a plethora of farmers' markets, so selling the produce isn't the problem; it's growing enough to meet demand. This possibly means using several backyards within a small area. Too much traveling makes crops suffer. The multiplot model requires drip irrigation on a timer, which is more expensive than spray irrigation, but saves the trouble of running around to all your plots four times a day for watering. Watering in the summer would be an impossible job.

The urban farmer needs one permanent spot to process crops. This means harvesting everything and then bringing it back to a place that has tables, a water supply and refrigerators or a walk-in cooler. An urban farm cooperative can help put this together; otherwise you'll have to have a garage for processing. This processing area needs to be close to all your plots as well.

The crops grown for this kind of farming are also different. No perennials can be grown or crops that take more than a year to mature, such as strawberries or asparagus. An excellent source of information for this is the SPIN model, which outlines exactly what crops to grow and how to do it based on profitability. It is based on a standard bed size, and each plot of land is dedicated to one crop. On one day of the week the farmer harvests one plot, and he or she moves to the next plot the next day. This produce is stored in a cooler, which can be built by the farmer, until the market day.

All of these are fairly standard farm issues, when the real challenge is zoning. City farms are facing conflicts, and unless the city has specifically allowed urban farming, it is probably illegal. The urban farmer is making the conscious choice to break city bylaws in the hope that the neighbors won't complain. There are two choices here—a tall fence can hide the backyard and make it impossible for anyone to even know what's going on or the farm can embrace the publicity. If the second option is chosen, be prepared to meet all the neighbors, offer them free vegetables, and become an ambassador for farming.

The Fruits of Our Labor

Our first CSA deliveries included baby carrots, something that had never been included in any local CSAs at that time of year, plus green onions, collard greens, radishes, and fresh herbs. The farm kept extremely detailed records so that I could tell how productive each square foot was and what varieties were the best. Even though I had grown up on a hobby farm in Montana, I soon realized that there was so much to know about each variety that I could have spent a lifetime studying and experimenting. There was no way I could have learned what I learned by driving around and just talking to farmers.

The most important lesson was learning exactly how much money it takes to grow food. We produced thousands of pounds of food, paid several farm laborers,

and educated eight full-time interns in that first year, but only because we were excellent marketers and sold directly. Almost all other farms have farm loans and mortgages to finance their operations and it takes years to break even. Farmers are selling food for half the actual cost and then getting subsidies and season advances to pay for the rest of it. In our case, the cost of production would only go down as we improved each year and had less investment in equipment.

It did alarm me that there was such a gap in the knowledge of so many of our customers. There were so many who were unappreciative of the tremendous amount of backbreaking work it takes to be a farmer, and in the first five years of starting a farm business, you are lucky to make more than a dollar an hour. I also faced the reality that most of my customers were affluent, despite our reasonable prices, and that they were fulfilling a whim. I had very mixed feelings about this, because I had wanted to supply everyone, no matter the income level.

There's a good reason I had such trouble finding a really successful small organic farm. It's so, so difficult. Most of it is hard physical labor, and the results are often completely out of your control. We lost crops to powdery mildew, bad seeds, too much rain, too much heat, and deer that defied the odds and jumped over nine feet of fencing. We also spent time marketing, delivering, doing customer service, accounting, and record keeping. But even through the heartbreak of failure, nothing could spoil the thrill of watching a tiny zucchini seed grow into

an enormous plant with leaves bigger than my head or biting into a sweet cherry tomato that burst with sugary flavor. The food didn't taste even remotely like the grocery store. We didn't even use any petroleum to grow it. This is something I can be proud of, and each farm and farmer that does this is securing the future just a little bit more. Just like the 1940s house with the little peach tree, every seed planted is a legacy.

Conclusion

During World War II, Victory Gardens were a necessity. The 1940s were tough and the government began rationing food as labor shortages made it difficult to produce enough fresh fruits and vegetables. To solve this problem, the US government began a highly successful propaganda campaign encouraging citizens to "Plant a Victory Garden." It was a simple concept: grow vegetables in your backyard to help win a war against oppression. Twenty million people answered the call, and by 1943, home gardens were producing an estimated 40 percent of the total produce of the nation. People took it one step further in their enthusiasm by planting in empty lots, city hall greens, and rooftops. Urban farming and food sovereignty is not a new idea. We've just forgotten all about how empowering and important it is to be responsible for our own food. Victory Gardens are making a comeback, and as anthropologist Devon Pena wrote in *Counterpunch*, "The return of urban farming echoes these monumental efforts of the past, but the new 'Victory Gardens' are about a victory over poverty, hunger, malnutrition, and the dissolution of community ties. The phenomenal success and rapid growth of urban farming has created extraordinary opportunities for food justice and an ecologically superior, community-based approach to reinvention of our current food system, which is dominated by unsustainable and inequitable industrial models and a profit-driven top-down corporate anti-nature and anti-worker rationality."

THE RIGHT TO EAT

Anyone who claims that a grassroots effort to grow food will not make an impact on our growing food crises is spouting propaganda for corporations. All the historical evidence we have points to small-scale agriculture in the hands of many as the solution, rather than large factory farming for the hands of few. We can see it in 1940s America, in Cuba, in Soviet Russia, in every economic crisis when food became too expensive or too scarce. The failures were those who tried to maintain control of the food supply and keep it out of the hands of citizens. Nazi Germany was one of those. Modern North America is becoming another. This change has to happen now. Everyone can grow something, unless you are living in a windowless box. Prisons and schools have acres of land that can be put to use. Cities own hundreds of acres of unused land that wastes away waiting for "economic development." Rural agriculture is often unsustainable and distributed far away on the other side of the world, and for what? So that a few investors can take a better vacation and send their kids to a better school than you can afford.

The tyrants that rule over our food supply will say and do anything to convince us that we can't grow food, that they do it better, that unless we give them more power our world will fall into chaos and starvation. Maybe they have convinced themselves that this is true. But we know better. Don't wait for change to happen. Get seeds right now. Make it happen.

"My friends, love is better than anger. Hope is better than fear. Optimism is better than despair. So let us be loving, hopeful and optimistic. And we'll change the world." —Jack Layton

Suggested Resources

Farmer Issues

Farmageddon the Movie: www.farmageddonmovie.com
Glynwood Institute: www.glynwood.org
La Via Campesina: www.viacampesina.org
Nyeleni: www.nyeleni.org
Rural Advancement International (USA): www.rafiusa.org

Urban Farm Projects

Growing Power: www.growingpower.org
Island Grains: www.islandgrains.com
Lawns to Loaves: lawnstoloaves.wordpress.com
Sweetwater Organics: www.sweetwater-organic.com

Farming Resources

Coolbot: www.storeitcold.com
Farm Hack: www.youngfarmers.org/practical/farm-hack
National Young Farmers' Coalition: www.youngfarmers.org
Open Source Ecology: www.opensourceecology.org
SPIN Farming: www.spinfarming.com
Young Agrarians: www.youngagrarians.org

Local Food

Locavores: www.locavores.com

Seattle Tilth: www.seattletilth.org

Urban Farm Hub: www.urbanfarmhub.org

Organics

Rodale Institute: www.rodaleinstitute.org/

Union of Concerned Scientists: www.ucsusa.org

USDA Soil Conservation Service: soils.usda.gov

Local Food

Local Harvest: www.localharvest.com

Slow Food: www.slowfood.com

Reclaiming Land

Detroit Works Project: www.detroitworksproject.com

Incredible Edible Todmorden: www.incredible-edible-todmorden.co.uk

Reclaim the Fields: www.reclaimthefields.org

The Land Is Ours: www.tlio.org.uk

Independent Certifiers

Certified Naturally Grown: www.naturallygrown.org

Kootenay Mountain Grown: www.klasociety.org/KMG.html

Montana Homegrown: www.homegrownmontana.org

Seed Saving

Heritage Seed Library (UK): www.gardenorganic.org.uk/hsl

Seeds of Diversity (Canada): www.seeds.ca

Seed Savers Exchange: www.seedsavers.org

Bibliography

Agence France-Presse. (2012, Feb.) Microsoft founder Bill Gates urges digital revolution against hunger. *Vancouver Sun.* www.vancouversun.com/story_print.html?id=6197206&sponsor= [Mar. 8, 2012]

Agriculture Department of the French Embassy. (2012, Jun.) Adapting the agriculture to a modern way of life. French Food in the US. www.french-foodintheus.org/spip.php?article3594 [Jun. 30, 2012]

American Farmland Trust (n.d.) What's Happening to Our Farmland. Farming on the Edge Report. www.farmland.org/resources/fote/default.asp [Jan. 17, 2012]

American Independent Business Association. (2012) The Multiplier Effect of Local Independent Business Ownership. www.amiba.net/resources/local-multiplier-effect [Aug. 1, 2012]

American Phytopathological Society. Emerging Diseases and Pathogens. APSnet. www.apsnet.org/members/apsleadership/comm/Pages/edpc.aspx [May 2, 2012]

Ballon, Marc. (2006, Jun. 23) A Harvest of Conflict: Did Anti-Semitism Take Root at the South Central Farm? *Jewish Journal.* www.cai-la.org/230606.html [Nov. 29, 2012]

Barclay, Eliza. (2012, Feb.) Judge Dismisses Organic Farmers' Case Against Monsanto. NPR *The Salt*. www.npr.org/blogs/thesalt/2012/02/27/147506542/judge-dismisses-organic-farmers-case-against-monsanto [Apr. 3, 2012]

Bass, Julie. (2012, Jul. 26) One year ago today. . . . OakParkHatesVeggies. http://oakparkhatesveggies.wordpress.com/2012/07/26/one-year-ago-today/ [Nov. 29, 2012]

BC Farm Industry Review Board. (2010) Stakeholder Submissions on the BC Egg Marketing Board New Producer Program Lottery Process. BCFIRB. www.firb.gov.bc.ca/reports/eggs/10_jul_16_stakeholder_submissions.pdf [Feb. 13]

Beaman, J. A., A. J. Johnson. (2006, Dec.) A Guide for New Distributors: Food Distribution Channel Overview. Oregon State University Extension. http://extension.oregonstate.edu/catalog/pdf/em/em8921.pdf [Jan. 30, 2012]

Becker, Dirk. (2012, Apr. 30) Compassion Farm Media Release. Mid-Island Sustainability and Stewardship Initiative. http://missimidisland.com/web_documents/apr30_june15.html [Nov. 29, 2012]

Bjerklie, David. (2003, Mar.) What Are Your Odds? *Time*. www.time.com/time/magazine/article/0,9171,1004582,00.html [Mar. 10, 2012]

Bondera, Melani, M. Query. (2006) Hawaiian Papaya: GMO Contaminated. Hawaii SEED. www.hawaiiseed.org/issues/papaya/papaya-contamination [Mar. 2012]

Bovine, The. (2009, Aug.) In 1999, 35 million small family plots produced 90% of Russia's potatoes, 77% of vegetables, 87% of fruits, 59% of meat, 49% of milk — way to go, people! The Bovine. http://thebovine.wordpress.

com/2009/08/09/in-1999-35-million-small-family-plots-produced-90-of-russias-potatoes-77-of-vegetables-87-of-fruits-59-of-meat-49-of-milk-way-to-go-people/ [Apr. 26, 2012]

Boyd, Robert. (2008, Dec.) Genetically Modified Hawaii. *Scientific American.* www.scientificamerican.com/article.cfm?id=genetically-modified-hawaii&page=2 [Mar. 9, 2012]

British Free Range Egg Producers Association. (May 2008) Free Range – the French way. *The Ranger.* www.theranger.co.uk/news/Free-Range-the-French-way_6449.html [Jul. 2, 2012]

Brown, Felicity. (2009, Aug.) Percentage of global population living in cities, by continent. *The Guardian.* www.guardian.co.uk/news/datablog/2009/aug/18/percentage-population-living-cities [Jul. 31, 2012]

Caldera, Sasha. (2011, Dec.) Indian cotton farmers maneuver between fair trade, Monsanto and debt in search of better life. *Vancouver Observer.* www.vancouverobserver.com/world/2011/12/15/indian-cotton-farmers-maneuver-between-fair-trade-monsanto-and-debt-search-better [Mar. 8, 2012]

Calumet Quarter. (2012) The Farm Bill: Ken Cook. University of Chicago Food Security Calumet Quarter. http://foodsecurity.uchicago.edu/interviews/farmbill/ [Jul. 7, 2012]

Canadian Cancer Society. (2010, May) Cancer: the leading cause of death in the country. Canadian Cancer Society. www.cancer.ca/Quebec/About%20us/Media%20centre/QC-Media%20releases/QC-Quebec%20media%20releases/QC_StatistiquesCanadiennesCancer_2010.aspx?sc_lang=en [Mar. 10, 2012]

Carman, Tim. (2011, Feb.) PCRM sues federal agencies over dietary guidelines. *Washington Post*. http://voices.washingtonpost.com/all-we-can-eat/food-politics/special-interest-groups-raise.html [Jul. 25, 2012]

Centers for Disease Control and Prevention (CDC). (2007) Foodborne Active Surveillance Network (FoodNet) Population Survey Atlas of Exposures. Atlanta, Georgia: U.S. Department of Health and Human Services, Centers for Disease Control and Prevention, 2006–2007. www.cdc.gov/foodnet/surveys/FoodNetExposureAtlas0607_508.pdf [May 16, 2012]

— (2012, Feb.) Majority of dairy-related disease outbreaks linked to raw milk. Centers for Disease Control and Prevention. [May 16, 2012]

— (2011, Nov.) Raw milk questions and answers. Centers for Disease Control and Prevention. [Nov. 29, 2012]

Certified Naturally Grown. (n.d.) About CNG. Certified Naturally Grown. www.naturallygrown.org/about-cng [Apr. 22, 2012]

Chambers, John. (2000, Apr.) *The Oxford Companion to American Military History*. Oxford University Press. p. 725. http://books.google.com/books?id=_Rzy_yNMKbcC&pg=PA725#v=onepage&q&f=false [Aug. 10, 2012]

Chao, E., K. Utgoff. (2006, May) 100 Years of U.S. Consumer Spending: Data for the Nation, New York City, and Boston. Bureau of Labor Statistics. www.bls.gov/opub/uscs/report991.pdf [May 3, 2012]

City of Vancouver. (2009) Food Policy in Vancouver: A Short History. City of Vancouver: Community Services. http://vancouver.ca/commsvcs/social-planning/initiatives/foodpolicy/policy/history.htm [Jun. 13, 2012]

BIBLIOGRAPHY

Clancy, Kate. (2006, Mar.) Greener Pastures: How grass-fed beef and milk contribute to healthy eating. Union of Concerned Scientists. www.ucsusa.org/assets/documents/food_and_agriculture/greener-pastures.pdf [Nov. 29, 2012]

Coleman-Jensen, Alisha, M. Nord, M. Andrews, S. Carlson (2011, Sept.) Household Food Security in the United States 2010. USDA. www.ers.usda.gov/publications/err-economic-research-report/err125.aspx

Collins, Harry. (2000) Terminator Technology Not Terminated. Agra/Industrial Biotechnology Legal Letter, January 2000, Vol. 1, No. 4

Colorado Farm to Market. (2012) General Licensing Requirements. Colorado Farm to Market. http://cofarmtomarket.com/food-regulations-licensing/general-licensing-requirements/ [Nov. 28, 2012]

Cornell University (1997, Aug. 12). U.S. Could Feed 800 Million People With Grain That Livestock Eat, Cornell Ecologist Advises. Cornell Science News. www.news.cornell.edu/releases/aug97/livestock.hrs.html [Jul. 12, 2012]

Coyne, Andrew. (2011, Aug. 15) The $25,000 cow. *Macleans*. www2.macleans.ca/2011/08/15/the-25000-cow/ [Nov. 28, 2012]

Credit Suisse. (2010, Oct.) Global Wealth Report. Credit Suisse Research Institute. http://thewisebuck.com/wp-content/uploads/2010/10/credit_suisse_global_wealth_report1.pdf [Jul. 3, 2012]

Crouch, Martha. (1998) How the Terminator terminates: an explanation for the non-scientists of a remarkable patent for killing second generation seeds of crop plants. The Edmonds Institute. www.psrast.org/terminexpl.htm [Aug. 15, 2012]

Crouch, Patrick. (2011, Dec.) The New Agtivist: Edith Floyd is making a Detroit urban farm, empty lot by empty lot. http://grist.org/urban-agriculture/2011-12-08-new-agtivist-edith-floyd-is-making-an-urban-farm-lot-by-lot/ [June 14, 2012]

Curtis, Deborah, A. Dickman, J.D., R. Horton, J. Brown, J. Slaske, C. Crother. (2005, Feb.) The Landscape of a Growing Southeastern Wisconsin. www.publicpolicyforum.org/sites/default/files/LandUseReport.pdf [Aug. 1, 2012]

Daniel, C.R., A.J. Cross, C. Koebnick, R. Sinha. (2011, Apr.) Trends in meat consumption in the USDA. Public Health Nutrition, U.S. National Library of Medicine. www.ncbi.nlm.nih.gov/pubmed/21070685 [Jul. 25, 2012]

Danielson, Dar. (2012, May) USDA responds to Grassley's comments on closing of beef processing plants. Radio Iowa. www.radioiowa.com/2012/05/09/u-s-d-a-responds-to-grassleys-comments-on-closing-of-beef-processing-plants/ [May 11, 2012]

Dare, Stephen. (2012, May) Reinventing urban agriculture. News 4 Ajax. www.news4jax.com/news/Reinventing-urban-agriculture/-/475880/10542146/-/item/2/-/j77hqsz/-/index.html [June 2, 2012]

Darré, Richard. (1940) Secret Nazi Speech: Reich Minister Darré Discusses the World's Future Under German Rule. *Life*. Pp. 43–44.

Davidson, Kate. (2011, Dec.) Blotting — Not Squatting — In Detroit Neighborhoods. www.npr.org/2011/12/05/142341520/blotting-not-squatting-in-detroit-neighborhoods [June 14, 2012]

BIBLIOGRAPHY

Davis, Donald. (2009, Feb.) Eating Your Veggies: Not As Good For You? *Time.* www.time.com/time/health/article/0,8599,1880145,00.html [Jan. 25, 2012]

De La Hamaide, Sybille. (2012, Mar.) French farmers, seedmakers appeal government GMO ban. Reuters. www.reuters.com/article/2012/03/29/us-france-gmo-idUSBRE82S0ZD20120329 [Jul. 2, 2012]

De Schutter, Olivier. (2010, Oct.) Access to Land the Right to Food. United Nations Special Rapporteur on the Right to Food. www.srfood.org/images/stories/pdf/officialreports/20101021_access-to-land-report_en.pdf [Jan. 19, 2012]

Detroit Works Project. (2010, Dec.) Policy Audit Topic: Urban Agriculture + Food Security. *Phase 1: Research and Priorities.* http://detroitworksproject.com/wp-content/uploads/policy_audits/101217_AECOM_1_Policy_Audit_Urban_Ag.pdf [Jan. 21, 2012]

Dietz, Kim. (2005, Aug.) Letter to Arthur Neal, Director of the National Organic Program. USDA. www.ams.usda.gov/AMSv1.0/getfile?dDocName =STELPRDC5061730 [Aug. 26, 2012]

District of Lantzville. (2011, Sept. 23) Urban Food Garden Committee Final Report. District of Lantzville. www.lantzville.ca/cms/wpattachments/wpID560atID3434.pdf [Nov. 29, 2012]

Economic Research Service. (2011, Dec.) State Fact Sheets: United States. USDA. www.ers.usda.gov/StateFacts/US.htm [Jan. 18, 2012]

Eide, Asbjørn. (2008) The Right to Food and the Impact of Liquid Biofuels (Agrofuels). FAO: Right to Food. www.fao.org/righttofood/publi08/Right_to_Food_and_Biofuels.pdf [Jul. 16, 2012]

Environmental Protection Agency. (n.d.) Ag 101: Demographics. EPA. www.epa.gov/agriculture/ag101/demographics.html [Feb. 18, 2012]

— (n.d.) General Information on Concentrated Feedlot Operations. EPA. http://cfpub.epa.gov/npdes/afo/info.cfm [Feb. 1, 2012]

— (n.d.) Major Crops Grown in the United States. EPA. www.epa.gov/oecaagct/ag101/cropmajor.html [Jul. 31, 2012]

European Food Safety Authority. (2007) Report of the Task Force on Zoonoses Data Collection on the Analysis of the baseline study on the prevalence of Salmonella in holdings of laying hen flocks of Gallus gallus. The EFSA Journal 97. www.efsa.europa.eu/EFSA/efsa_locale-1178620753812_1178620761896.htm [May 15, 2012]

Fallon, Amy. (2011, Feb.) 'Local' food labeling misleads consumers, regulator reveals. The Guardian. www.guardian.co.uk/environment/2011/feb/26/local-food-labelling-misleading-consumers [Jan. 27, 2012]

Fankhauser, David PhD. (1999, Sept.) Hazards of Genetically Modified Crops and Foods. University of Cincinnati Clermont College. http://biology.clc.uc.edu/fankhauser/Society/Gen_Engnrg7Oct99.html [June 9, 2012]

— (2002) Hazards of Genetically Modified Foods. University of Cincinnati Clermont College. http://biology.clc.uc.edu/fankhauser/Society/Gen_Engnrg7Oct99.html [Mar. 5, 2012]

FAO. (2006, Jun.) Country Profile: Food Security Indicators Cuba. Food and Agriculture Organization of the UN. www.fao.org/fileadmin/templates/

ess/documents/food_security_statistics/country_profiles/eng/Cuba_E.pdf [Aug. 4, 2012]

(2012) Can organic farmers produce enough food for everybody? FAO. www.fao.org/organicag/oa-faq/oa-faq7/en/ [Jan. 31, 2012]

— Food Security. FAO Policy Brief. ftp://ftp.fao.org/es/ESA/policybriefs/ pb_02.pdf [Jul. 11, 2012]

— (2009) International treaty on plant genetic resources for food and agriculture.   FAO   ftp://ftp.fao.org/docrep/fao/011/i0510e/i0510e.pdf [Aug. 12, 2012]

FarmForward. (n.d.) Factory Farming. FarmForward. www.farmforward. com/farming-forward/factory-farming [Feb. 1, 2012]

Fawthrop, Tom. (2004, Nov.) Agent Orange Victims Sue Monsanto. *CorpWatch*. www.corpwatch.org/article.php?id=11638 [Aug. 10, 2012]

FDA. (2012, May) The New Food Safety Modernization Act. Food and Drug Administration. www.fda.gov/food/foodsafety/fsma/default.htm [May 14, 2012]

— (2012, Apr.) Progress Report. Food and Drug Administration. www. fda.gov/Food/FoodSafety/FSMA/ucm255893.htm [May 16, 2012]

Federal Ministry of Food, Agriculture and Consumer Protection. (2012, Jan.) Organic Farming in Germany. www.bmelv.de/SharedDocs/Standardartikel/ EN/Agriculture/OrganicFarming/OrganicFarmingInGermany.html [Jul. 3, 2012]

Fleischer, Doris. (2001) *The Disability Rights Movement: From Charity to Confrontation.* Temple University Press. p. 178. http://books.google.com/books?id=3t84d8tLEVcC&pg=PA178#v=onepage&q&f=false [Aug. 10, 2012]

Folsom Jr., Burton. (2006, Apr.) The Origin of American Farm Subsidies. *The Freeman.* Foundation for Economic Education. www.fee.org/pdf/thefreeman/0604Folsom.pdf [Jan. 14, 2012]

Food for Maine's Future. (2012, Apr.) Internal Dept. of Ag Emails Raise Questions About Motivations in Farmer Brown Case. Sourcewatch. www.sourcewatch.org/images/f/f7/Food_for_Maine%27s_Future_Press_Release.pdf [Jun. 12, 2012]

Forbes. (n.d.) Robert T. Frayley. Forbes People. http://people.forbes.com/profile/robert-t-fraley/54822 [May 7, 2012]

French Presidency of the G-20. Commodity Price Volatility. G-20. www.g20-g8.com/g8-g20/g20/english/priorities-for-france/the-priorities-of-the-french-presidency/sheets/commodity-price-volatility.353.html [Jul.12, 2012]

Frye, Russell, E. White. (2007, Mar.) CREEKSTONE FARMS PREMIUM BEEF, L.L.C.,Plaintiff, v. U.S.DEPARTMENTOFAGRICULTURE,etal.,Defendants. http://scholar.google.com/scholar_case?case=10133437571583048889 [Jun. 11, 2012]

Fullbright, Lori. (2012, June) Woman Sues City of Tulsa for Cutting Down Her Edible Garden. Newson6.com. www.newson6.com/story/18802728/woman-sues-city-of-tulsa-for-cutting-down-her-edible-garden [June 20, 2012]

Gaffney, Neil. (2011, Dec.) Northeastern Grocery Chain Recalls Ground Beef Products Due to Possible *Salmonella* Contamination. USDA Food

BIBLIOGRAPHY

Safety and Inspection Service. www.fsis.usda.gov/News_&_Events/ Recall_100_2011_Release/index.asp [Feb. 7, 2012]

Gallagher, James. (2012, Jan.) Processed meat 'linked to pancreatic cancer'. *BBC News: Health*. www.bbc.co.uk/news/health-16526695 [Mar. 10, 2012]

Gascape Publications. (1997) Health Effects of Dioxins. State of California. www.gascape.org/index%20/Health%20effects%20of%20Dioxins.html [Aug. 9, 2012]

Geographical. (2011, Dec.) The town that wants to feed itself. *Geographical.* www.geographical.co.uk/Magazine/Todmorden_-_Dec_11.html [Jul. 20, 2012]

Gillam, Cary. (2011, Feb.) Scientist warns on safety of Monsanto's Roundup. Reuters. www.reuters.com/article/2011/02/24/us-monsanto-roundup-idUS-TRE71N4XN20110224 [May 2, 2012]

Godo, Yoshihisa. (2007) The Puzzle of Small Farming in Japan. Australia-Japan Research Centre. www.eastasiaforum.org/testing/eaber/sites/default/files/documents/AJRC_Godo_07.pdf [June 29, 2012]

Gold, L.S., T.H. Slone, B.N. Ames, N.B. Manley. Pesticide Residues in Food and Cancer Risk: A Critical Analysis. *Handbook of Pesticide Toxicology*, Second Edition (R. Krieger, ed.), San Diego, CA: Academic Press, pp. 799–843 (2001).

Goldman Environmental Prize. (2012) Sofia Gatica. Goldman Environmental Prize. www.goldmanprize.org/recipient/sofia-gatica [May 4, 2012]

Goode, Jamie. (n.d.) Terroir revisited: towards a working definition. Wineanorak.com. www.foodtree.com/profile/source?id=10146&map=false &images=false&connections=false&activity=true [Jan. 27, 2012]

Greater Victoria Compost Education Centre. (n.d.) Composting Fact Sheet Series. Greater Victoria Compost Education Centre. www.compost.bc.ca/learn/howto.htm [Jan. 23, 2012]

Greene, Catherine, E. Slattery, W. McBride. (2010, Jun.) America's Organic Farmers Face Issues and Opportunities. USDA *Amber Waves*. www.ers.usda.gov/AmberWaves/june10/Features/AmericasOrganicFarmers.htm [Apr. 25, 2012]

Greger, Michael, M.D. (2012, May) Mad Cow California: What Is Atypical BSE? *The Huffington Post*. www.huffingtonpost.com/michael-greger-md/mad-cow-disease_b_1476074.html [June 11, 2012]

Grist. (2005) Fight over synthetic ingredients splits organics community. *Grist*. http://grist.org/food/organics/ [Apr. 19, 2012]

Groceteria. (n.d.) A Quick History of the Supermarket. Groceteria. Retrieved from www.groceteria.com/about/a-quick-history-of-the-supermarket/ [Feb. 11, 2012]

Gumpert, David. (2011, Dec.) Amid Sheriff-DOFJ Warnings, Pullback on Grand Jury Investigation of IN Dairy Farmer; Raw Milk Freedom Riders Push Further on Interstate Milk Prohibition. The Complete Patient. www.thecompletepatient.com/article/2011/december/7/amid-sheriff-dofj-warnings-pullback-grand-jury-investigation-dairy-farmer [Nov. 29, 2012]

— (2007, Apr.) Back in Biz, Thanks to Very Vocal Customers. *Business Week*. www.businessweek.com/smallbiz/content/apr2007/sb20070426_582900.htm [May 23, 2012]

Gurian-Sherman, Doug. (2009, Apr.) Failure to Yield: Evaluating the Performance of Genetically Engineered Crops. Union of Concerned Scientists. www.ucsusa.org/assets/documents/food_and_agriculture/failure-to-yield.pdf [Mar. 8, 2012]

Hall, Kevin D., J. Guo, M. Dore, C.C. Chow. (2009) The Progressive Increase of Food Waste in America and Its Environmental Impact. PLoS ONE 4(11): e7940. doi:10.1371/journal.pone.0007940 [Jul. 12, 2012]

Harada, Yutaka. (2012, Jan.) Can Japanese Farming Survive Liberalization. The Tokyo Foundation. www.tokyofoundation.org/en/articles/2011/farming-survive-liberalization [Jun. 29, 2012]

Harrison, John Arthur. (2003) The Nitrogen Cycle: Of Microbes and Men. *Visionlearning* Vol. EAS-2. www.visionlearning.com/library/module_viewer. php?mid=98 [Jan. 16, 2012]

Hartley, Sarah. (2011, Sept.) Todmorden attracts international interest for Incredible Edible. *The Guardian: The Northerner Blog.* Retrieved from www.guardian.co.uk/uk/the-northerner/2011/sep/26/incredible-edible-todmorden?newsfeed=true {Jan. 27, 2012]

Hauter, Wenonah. (2012, Feb.) Wenonah Hauter: Who Pays the 'Farm Bill'? [video file] www.youtube.com/watch?feature=player_embedded&v=bAp CXRqUMSw

Hills, M., L. Hall, P. Arnison, A. Good. (2010) Genetic use restriction technologies (GURTs): strategies to impede transgene movement. *TRENDS in Plant Science* Vol.12 No.4. www.cof.orst.edu/cof/teach/agbio2010/Other%20Readings/GURTS%20Rev%20Trends%20Pl%20Sci%202007. pdf [Mar. 13, 2012]

History Commons. (n.d.) Context of "July 6, 2001: USDA and Delta & Pine Land Conclude Negotations on Terminator Patent." www.historycommons.org/context.jsp?item=gm-142&scale=1#gm-142 [Aug. 15, 2012]

History Place. (2000) Irish Potato Famine. The History Place. Retrieved from www.historyplace.com/worldhistory/famine/

Howard, Philip. (n.d.) Organic Distribution & Retail Structure. Michigan State University. www.msu.edu/%7Ehowardp/organicdistributors.html [Apr. 17, 2012]

— (n.d.) Organic Processing Structure. Michigan State University. www.msu.edu/%7Ehowardp/organicindustry.html [Apr. 17, 2012]

Howell, Shea. (2012, Jul.) Land Misuse. The Michigan Citizen. http://michigancitizen.com/land-misuse-p11369-1.htm [Jul. 17, 2012]

Huber, Don. (2011, Mar.) Letter from Dr. Huber to European Commission. Farm and Ranch Freedom Alliance. http://farmandranchfreedom.org/huber-european-letter [May 2, 2012]

IFOAM. (n.d.) IFOAM PGS Database. IFOAM. www.ifoam.org/about_ifoam/standards/pgs_projects/pgs_projects/index.php [Apr. 23, 2012]

ISAAA. (2011) Q & A About Genetically Modified Crops. International Service for the Acquisition of Agri-Biotech Applications. www.isaaa.org/resources/publications/pocketk/1/default.asp [Feb. 7, 2012]

Jenkins, Colleen. (2011, Dec.) Butterball turkey facility search for abuse of birds. Reuters. www.reuters.com/article/2011/12/29/us-butterball-abuse-idUSTRE7BS16Q20111229 [Feb. 7, 2012]

BIBLIOGRAPHY

Jones, Montana. (2012, Jun.) Save Our Shropshires! Wholeearth Farmstudio. http://wholearth.com/shropshire-sheep [Jun. 9, 2012]

Kalish, Joe. (2011, Sept.) Farming Detroit. *Make.* http://blog.makezine. com/2011/09/09/farming-detroit/ [Jun. 19, 2012]

Kantor, Linda Scott, K. Lipton, A. Manchester, V. Oliveira. *FoodReview: From Farm to Table: The Economics of Food Safety; Estimating and Addressing America's Food Losses.* www.ers.usda.gov/publications/foodreview/jan1997/ jan97d.pdf [May 15, 2012]

Kerns, D.L., M.E. Matheron, J.C. Palumbo, C.A. Sanchez, D.W. Still, B.R. Tickes, K. Umeda, M.A. Wilcox. (1999, Feb.) Guidelines for Head Lettuce Production in Arizona. IPM Series Number 12. Publication number az1099. Cooperative Extension, College of Agriculture and Life Sciences, University of Arizona, Tucson, Arizona. http://cals.arizona.edu/ crops/vegetables/cropmgt/az1099.html [Apr. 17, 2012]

Killman, Scott. USDA Cracks Down on Synthetic Fatty Acids in Organic Milk. *The Wall Street Journal.* http://online.wsj.com/article/SB1000142405 27487044647045752087521646666686.html [Apr. 18, 2012]

Kindi, K., L. Layton. (2009, Jul.) Integrity of Federal 'Organic' Label Questioned. *Washington Post.* www.washingtonpost.com/wp-dyn/content/ article/2009/07/02/AR2009070203365.html [Apr. 13, 2012]

Kimani, Mary. (n.d.) Women claim legal right to land access. *United Nations African Renewal.* www.un.org/ecosocdev/geninfo/afrec/newrels/221-women-claim-land-rights.html [Jan. 19, 2012]

Knuth, Lidija, M. Vidar. (2011) Constitutional and Legal Protection of the Right to Food Around the World. Food and Agriculture Organization of the

United Nations. www.fao.org/righttofood/publi11/constitutional_2011. pdf [Jul. 24, 2012]

Koont, Sinan. (2004, Jan.) Food Security in Cuba. *Monthly Review, Vol. 55, Issue 08.* http://monthlyreview.org/2004/01/01/food-security-in-cuba [Aug. 4, 2012]

LaLande, Jeff. (2005) A New Century: Last Land Rush and Later Boom/ Bust Times: Dry-Farm Homesteading Boom and Failure, 1905 – 1920. The Oregon History Project. www.ohs.org/education/oregonhistory/narratives/ subtopic.cfm?subtopic_id=465 [Jan. 19, 2012]

Lang, Susan. (2005, Jul.) Organic farming produces same corn and soybean yields as conventional farms, but consumes less energy and no pesticides, study finds. Cornell University News Service. www.news.cornell.edu/stories/July05/organic.farm.vs.other.ssl.html [Apr. 25, 2012]

Larkin, Catherine. (2006, Jul.) U.S. to Reduce Mad-Cow Testing After Few Cases Found. *Bloomberg.* Retrieved from www.bloomberg.com/apps/ news?pid=newsarchive&sid=a2_DTcbM8BZA&refer=japan [Feb. 6, 2012]

Lin, C.-T. Jordan, R. A. Morales, and K. Ralston. (1997, Jan.) *FoodReview: Food Safety; Raw and Undercooked Eggs: A Danger of Salmonellosis.* www. ers.usda.gov/publications/foodreview/jan1997/jan97d.pdf [May 15, 2012] [May 15, 2012]

Lovett, Ian. (2011, Aug.) Raw Food Coop Is Raided in California. *The New York Times.* www.nytimes.com/2011/08/05/us/05raw.html [May 23, 2012]

Lowdermilk, Dr. W. C. (1948, Feb.) Conquest of the Land Through Seven Thousand Years. USDA Natural Resource Conservation Service. http:// journeytoforever.org/farm_library/Lowd/Lowd1.html [Jan. 14, 2012]

BIBLIOGRAPHY

Lowenstein, Kate. (2011, Oct.) Not safe to eat: Three foods to avoid. CNN Health. www.cnn.com/2011/10/12/health/food-poisoning-protection-guide/index.html [May 16, 2012]

Lutzenberger, José. (1998) The Absurdity of Modern Agriculture – From Chemical Fertilizers and Agropoisons to Biotechnology. Fundação Gaia. www.fgaia.org.br/texts/e-biotech.html [Jul. 2, 2012]

Maloney, Field. (2006, Mar.) Is Whole Foods Wholesome? *Slate.* www.slate.com/articles/arts/culturebox/2006/03/is_whole_foods_wholesome.html [Apr. 17, 2012]

Marcus, Erik. (2011, Dec.) Will the Butterball raid yield any real results? *Grist.* http://grist.org/factory-farms/2011-12-29-will-butterball-raid-yield-any-real-results/ [Feb. 7, 2012]

Markley, Kristen. (2012, Dec.) Food Safety and Liability Insurance: Emerging Issues for Farmers and Institutions. www.foodsecurity.org/pub/Food_Safety_and_Liability_Ins-EmergingIssues.pdf [May 14, 2012]

Mashima, Yoshitaka. (2007, Feb.) Rice production and agricultural policies in Japan. Forum for Food Sovereignity 2007. www.nyeleni.org/spip.php?article26 [Jul. 4, 2012]

McGarity, Thomas. (2012, Nov.) Critical Food Safety Rules Still in Regulatory Limbo, Now Stuck at White House for a Full Year. Civil Eats. http://civileats.com/2012/11/28/critical-food-safety-rules-still-in-regulatory-limbo-now-stuck-at-white-house-for-a-full-year/ [Nov. 28, 2012]

213

McKenzie, Ross. (2003, May) Soil pH and Plant Nutrition. Government of Alberta Agriculture and Rural Development. www1.agric.gov.ab.ca/$department/deptdocs.nsf/all/agdex6607 [Jan. 16, 2012]

Miller, Kevin. (2011, Nov.) Farmers, consumers rally to support man's selling of 'raw milk.' *Bangor Daily News.* http://bangordailynews.com/2011/11/18/news/hancock/farmers-consumers-rally-to-support-man's-selling-of-'raw-milk'/ [May 21, 2012]

Milstein, Michel. (2009, Oct.) 6 Radical Solutions for U.S. Southwest's Peak Water Problem. *Popular Mechanics.* www.popularmechanics.com/science/environment/4287425 [Apr. 17, 2012]

Mitchell, Donald. (2008, Apr.) A Note on Rising Food Prices. World Bank. http://image.guardian.co.uk/sys-files/Environment/documents/2008/07/10/Biofuels.PDF [Jul. 16, 2012]

Monsanto. (2008) Farmer Suicides in India – Is There a Link to Bt Cotton? Monsanto News & Views. www.monsanto.com/newsviews/Pages/india-farmer-suicides.aspx [Mar.15, 2012]

— (n.d.) Is Monsanto Going to Develop "Terminator" Seeds? Monsanto News & Views. www.monsanto.com/newsviews/Pages/terminator-seeds.aspx [Aug. 15, 2012]

— (n.d.) Saved Seed and Farmer Lawsuits. Monsanto News and Views. www.monsanto.com/newsviews/Pages/saved-seed-farmer-lawsuits.aspx [Apr. 3, 2012]

BIBLIOGRAPHY

National Agricultural Statistics Service. (2007) 2007 Census of Agriculture: Farmers by Age. USDA. www.agcensus.usda.gov/Publications/2007/ Online_Highlights/Fact_Sheets/farmer_age.pdf [Jan. 17, 2012]

National Association of Realtors. (2003) FAQ: What percentage of disposable income is spent on housing-related expenses? Realtor.org. www.realtor. org/library/referral/whatpercentageofdisposableinco [Feb. 11, 2012]

National Cancer Institute. (2012) Agricultural Health Study. National Institute of Health. www.cancer.gov/cancertopics/factsheet/Risk/ahs [May 2, 2012]

— (2008) Childhood Cancers. National Institute of Health. www.cancer. gov/cancertopics/factsheet/Sites-Types/childhood [Aug. 14, 2012]

— (2008, Dec.) New Tool Developed to Predict Colorectal Cancer Risk. National Institute of Health. www.cancer.gov/newscenter/pressreleases/2008/ colorectalriskmodel [Mar. 10, 2012]

— (2010, Sept.) Probability of Breast Cancer in American Women. National Institute of Health. www.cancer.gov/cancertopics/factsheet/detection /probability-breast-cancer [Mar. 10, 2012]

National Creutzfeldt-Jakob Disease Research and Surveillance Unit. (2011, Nov.) Current Data. www.cjd.ed.ac.uk/vcjdworld.htm. [Feb. 6, 2012]

National Organic Program. (2012, Jan.) National Organic Standards Board. Agricultural Marketing Service. www.ams.usda.gov/AMSv1.0/ams.fetch-TemplateData.do?template=TemplateG&navID=NationalOrganicProgram &leftNav=NationalOrganicProgram&page=NOSBFormerMembers&desc ription=NOSB%20Former%20Members&acct=nop [Apr. 22, 2012]

National Weather Service. (2010, Aug.) The Black Sunday Dust Storm of 14 April 1935. NWS Norman, OK Weather Forecast Office. www.srh.noaa. gov/oun/?n=blacksunday [Aug. 7, 2012]

Natural Resource Conservation Service. (n.d.) Helping People Understand Soils: Ten Key Messages. USDA. http://urbanext.illinois.edu/soil/sellsoil/ sellsoil.pdf [Jan. 14, 2012]

Natural Resource Defense Council. (2005, Aug.) Pollution from Giant Livestock Farms Threatens Public Health. NRDC. www.nrdc.org/water/ pollution/nspills.asp [Feb. 6, 2012]

Neild, Jeff. (2012, Jan.) BC Farmer Saved from Jail by Voters. *Treehugger*. www.treehugger.com/sustainable-agriculture/bc-farmer-saved-jail-voters. html [Jun. 2, 2012]

Nelson, Cary. (n.d.) About the Dust Bowl. Modern American Poetry, Department of English, University of Illinois. www.english.illinois.edu/ maps/depression/depression.htm [Jan. 18, 2012]

Nguyen, Linda. (2011, Dec.) Raw-milk farmer Michael Schmidt appeals convictions for illegal cow-share program. *National Post*. http://news. nationalpost.com/2011/12/19/raw-milk-farmer-michael-schmidt-appeals-convictions-for-illegal-cow-share-program/ [May 21, 2012]

NOAA National Climatic Data Center. (2012, Jul.) State of the Climate: Drought for June 2012. NOAA National Climatic Data Center. www.ncdc. noaa.gov/sotc/drought/ [Aug. 7, 2012]

Nordgen. (n.d.) Agreement Between (Depositor) and the Royal Norwegian Ministry of Agriculture and Food Concerning the Deposit of Seeds in the Svalbard Global Seed Vault. Nordgen. www.nordgen.org/sgsv/scope/sgsv/ files/SGSV_Deposit_Agreement.pdf [Aug. 17, 2012]

Nove, Alec. (1966) *The Soviet Economy: An Introduction.* New York: Praeger.

Now. (2004, Jun.) Who is the Middle Class? PBS. www.pbs.org/now/politics/middleclassoverview.html [Jan. 27, 2012]

Observer, The. (2003, Jul.) Just how old are the 'fresh' fruit and vegetables we eat? *The Guardian*. www.guardian.co.uk/lifeandstyle/2003/jul/13/foodanddrink.features18 [Jan. 25, 2012]

Oosting, Jonathan. (2011, Nov.) State Senator looks to amend Michigan Right to Farm Act, let Detroit regulate urban farming. MLive. www.mlive.com/news/detroit/index.ssf/2011/11/state_legislator_looks_to_amen.html [Jun. 15, 2012]

Organic Consumers Association. (2000, Mar.) BioDemocracy News #25 Organic Standards Revisited. OCA. www.organicconsumers.org/newsletter/biod25.cfm [Apr. 18, 2012]

Organic Trade Association. (n.d.) Export Study – Chapter 3: Europe. OTA. www.ota.com/organic/mt/export_chapter3.html [Jul. 2, 2012]

— Lawsuit Chronology. OTA. www.ota.com/LawsuitChronology.html [Apr. 20, 2012]

Parker, Hilary. (2010, Mar.) A sweet problem: Princeton researchers find that high-fructose corn syrup prompts considerably more weight gain. *News at Princeton*. www.princeton.edu/main/news/archive/S26/91/22K07/ [Jan. 31, 2012]

Parker, Susie. (2006, Feb.) How poultry producers are ravaging the rural South. *Grist*. http://grist.org/food/parker1/ [Feb. 10, 2012]

Parsa, H.G., J. Self, D. Njite, T. King. (2005) Why Restaurants Fail. Cornell University. www.econ.ucsb.edu/~tedb/Courses/Ec1F07/restaurantsfail.pdf [Feb. 18, 2012]

PCRM. (2001) PCRM Wins USDA Lawsuit. PCRM. www.pcrm.org/good-medicine/2001/winter/pcrm-wins-usda-lawsuit [Jul. 25, 2012]

Pena, Devon. (2012, Aug.) Urban Farms or Myths? *Counterpunch*. www.counterpunch.org/2012/08/02/urban-farms-or-myths/ [Aug. 6, 2012]

Petzel, Andrea. (2010, Aug.) Urban Agriculture Ordinance: Ordinance 123378. Seattle Department of Planning and Development. www.seattle. gov/dpd/cms/groups/pan/@pan/@plan/@urbanagriculture/documents/ web_informational/dpdp020184.pdf [June 19, 2012]

Philphott, Tom. (2011, Jul.) Wait, Did the USA Just Deregulate All New Genetically Modified Crops. *Mother Jones.* www.motherjones.com/environ- ment/2011/07/usda-deregulate-roundup-gmo-tom-philpott [Mar. 5, 2012]

— (2010, Oct.) Obama taps food-industry exec for top ag-research post. Grist. http://grist.org/politics/2010-10-01-obama-taps-food-industry-exec- to-top-ag-research-post/ [May 8, 2012]

Picard, André. (2012, Apr.) Ontario sheep kidnappers say infected flock is in 'protective custody.' *The Globe and Mail.* www.theglobeandmail.com/ news/national/ontario-sheep-kidnappers-say-infected-flock-is-in-protec- tive-custody/article2417448/ [Jun. 9, 2012]

Pickrell, John. (2004, July) Ancient Skeleton Collection Yields Cancer Clues. *National Geographic News.* http://news.nationalgeographic.com/ news/2004/07/0713_040713_skeletoncancer.html [Aug. 14, 2012]

Piggly Wiggly. (n.d.) Where it began . . . Piggly Wiggly. www.pigglywiggly. com/about-us [Feb. 11, 2012]

Pinstrup-Andersen, Per. (2002, Mar.) Towards a Sustainable Food System: What Will it Take? International Food Policy Research Institute. www.ifpri. cgiar.org/sites/default/files/pubs/pubs/articles/2002/pinstrup02_01.pdf [Apr. 24, 2012]

Polman, Paul, D. Servitje. (2012, Jun.) The global challenge of food and nutrition security. *Washington Post: Opinions.* www.washingtonpost.com/ opinions/the-global-challenge-of-food-and-nutrition-security/2012/06/17/ gJQAWse1jV_story.html [Jul. 12, 2012]

Pothukuchi, Kami. (2011, May) The Detroit Food Systems Report, 2009–2010. Detroit Food Policy Council. www.clas.wayne.edu/multimedia/user-content/File/SEED/2DetFoodReport_2009-10lores.pdf [Jun. 15, 2012]

Putnam, J.J., J. Allshouse. (1999, Apr.) Food Consumption, Prices and Expenditures, 1970–97. USDA. www.ers.usda.gov/Publications/sb965/ [Feb. 10, 2012]

Radford, Leslie. (2006, Dec. 22) The Winter Harvest of the South Central Farmers. CounterCurrents. www.countercurrents.org/radford221206.htm [Nov. 29, 2012]

Raftis, Lindsay. (2009, Aug.) Production and Consumption of Food Calories in the Lower Mainland of British Columbia: Identifying Strategies and Barriers to a Self-reliant Regional Food System. *Foundational Research Bulletin.* www.dcs.sala.ubc.ca/docs/sxd_frb_food_self_reliance_sec.pdf [Apr. 24, 2012]

Realfoodrights. (2010, July) FDA Raid on Raw Milk: Rawsome Food Club. [video file] www.youtube.com/watch?v=X2jgpGyyQW8 [May 28, 2012]

Regional Food Policy Council, University of Washington. (2011, Jun.) Food Production: Urban Agriculture. University of Washington Department of Urban Design and Planning. http://courses.washington.edu/studio67/psrc-food/Food_studio_docs/Vol04_Urban_Ag.pdf [June. 21, 2012]

Ries, Lynn , Smith, M.A., Gurney, J.G., Linet, M., Tamra, T., Young, J.L., Bunin, G.R. (eds). (1999) Cancer Incidence and Survival among Children and Adolescents: United States SEER Program 1975–1995. National Cancer Institute, SEER Program. NIH Pub. No. 99-4649. Bethesda, MD.

Right Diagnosis. (2012) Statistics about E-coli poisoning. Right Diagnosis. www.rightdiagnosis.com/e/e_coli_food_poisoning/stats.htm [Aug. 28, 2012]

Robertson, Lori. (2009, Mar.) Illegal Backyard Garden? FactCheck.org. www.factcheck.org/2009/03/illegal-backyard-garden/ [May 14, 2012]

Rodale. (n.d.) The Farm Systems Trial. Rodale Institute. www.rodaleinstitute.org/fst30years [Apr. 25, 2012]

Roper Public Affairs. (2004, Apr.) Food and Farming 2004. NOP World. www.organicvalley.coop/pdf/roper_survey.pdf [Feb. 8, 2012]

Ruiz, Rebecca. Are You Eating Too Much Meat? *Forbes*. www.forbes.com/2009/03/24/eating-red-meat-lifestyle-health-red-meat-study.html [Jul. 25, 2012]

Rural Advancement Foundation International (2000, May) Terminator Two Years Later: RAFI Update on Terminator/Traitor Technology. Action Group on Erosion, Technology and Concentration. www.etcgroup.org/upload/publication/324/01/other_rafiupdate.pdf [Mar. 15, 2012]

Sakalauskas, L. (2010, Aug.) 2010 Quota Distribution Policy. BC Egg Marketing Board. www.bcegg.com/files/documents/Policy10-03submission_Quotaallocation2010_FINAL.pdf [Feb. 13, 2012]

Sanchez-Cuenca, Jordi. (2010, Sept.) The Origin of Permaculture in Cuba. Polis. www.thepolisblog.org/search?q=urban+agriculture [Aug. 4, 2012]

Schafer, Melissa. (2006, May) The Sustainable Food and Agricultural Movement in Munich, Germany. Joint Organic Congress, Odense, Denmark. http://orgprints.org/7528/2/7528_Shafer.pdf [Jul. 4, 2012]

Schmidt, Sarah. (2012, May) UN envoy blasts Canada for 'self-righteous' attitude over hunger, poverty. *National Post*. http://news.nationalpost.com/2012/05/15/un-envoy-blasts-canada-for-self-righteous-attitude-over-hunger-poverty/ [Jul. 17, 2012]

Schneider, Roger. (2011, Dec.) Middlebury Dairy Farmer Stands Up to the FDA. *Goshen News*. http://goshennews.com/local/x1996142009/Middlebury-dairy-farmer-Sheriff-stand-up-to-FDA [May 21, 2012]

Schutzbank, Marc. (2010) Vegetable Vancouver 2010, An Urban Farming Census. www.cityfarmer.org/UF2010.pdf [Jun. 14, 2012]

Scott, Brett. (2011, Jun.) A guide to food speculation: how to argue with a banker. *The Ecologist.* www.theecologist.org/News/news_analysis/931513/a_guide_to_food_speculation_how_to_argue_with_a_banker.html [Jan. 31, 2012]

Seattle Office of Sustainability and Development. (2011) City Wide Accomplishments 2008–Present. Local Food Action Initiative. www.seattle.gov/environment/documents/LFAI_CityAccomp2008-2011.pdf [June 19, 2012]

Seeds of Change. (2008) Heritage Seed Library: Seed Saving Guidelines. Garden Organic. www.gardenorganic.org.uk/members/seed_saving/index.php [Apr. 3, 2012]

Shapiro, Robert. (1999) Open Letter from Monsanto CEO Robert B. Shapiro to Rockefeller Foundation President Gordon Conway and Others. Monsanto News & Views. www.monsanto.com/newsviews/Pages/monsanto-ceo-to-rockefeller-foundation-president-gordon-conway-terminator-technology.aspx [Aug. 15, 2012]

Sharaskin, Leonid. (2008, May) The Socioeconomic and Cultural Significance of Food Gardening in the Vladimir Region of Russia. University of Missouri-Columbia. www.primaryagriculture.com/dissertation.pdf [Aug. 27, 2012]

Shaw, Steven. (2000, Jan.) Cheesy does it. *Solon.* www.salon.com/2000/01/28/cheese/ [Nov. 29, 2012]

Shropshiresheep.org (2011, Dec.) CFIA to slaughter healthy rare heritage sheep. Shropshiresheep.org. http://shropshiresheep.org/news-on-cfia-slaughter/ [Jun. 9, 2012]

Spector, David (2008, Apr.) Farming Without Farmers; J.I. Rodale and the American Organic Farming Movement. Columbia University Department of History. http://history.columbia.edu/resource-library/Spector_thesis.pdf [Apr. 13, 2012]

Spoerer, Mark. (2006) Guns and Butter – But No Margarine: The Impact of Nazi Agricultural and Consumption Policies on German Food Production and Consumption. XIV International Economic History Congress. www.helsinki.fi/iehc2006/papers3/Spoerer85.pdf [Jun. 26, 2012]

Sturm, Tom. (2012, Apr.) GMO Labeling Bill Stuck in Vermont Committee. *The Valley Advocate.* www.valleyadvocate.com/article.cfm?aid=14922 [Apr. 10, 2012]

Tennant, Michael. (2012, Jan.) Raw Milk Mandates. *The New American.* www.thenewamerican.com/economy/sectors/item/4389-raw-milk-mandates [May 21, 2012]

Thier, Dave. (2010, Sept.) Cabbagegate: Man Fined $5K for Home Garden. AOLNews. www.aolnews.com/2010/09/15/cabbagegate-ga-man-fined-5k-for-home-garden/ [May 31, 2012]

Tugel, A.J., A.M. Lewandowski, eds. (February 2001 — last update). Soil Biology Primer [online]. http://urbanext.illinois.edu/soil/SoilBiology/soil_biology_primer.htm [Jan. 14, 2012]

University of Wisconsin Cooperative Extension. (2011) Milwaukee County Agriculture: Value & Economic Impact. UW Extension. www.uwex.edu/ces/ag/wisag/documents/agimpactbrochMilwaukeeCoFINAL.pdf [Aug. 1, 2012]

U.S. Apple Association. (n.d.) Varieties. Consumers: All About Apples. www.usapple.org/consumers/all-about-apples/apple-varieties-and-apple-products/varieties [Feb. 27, 2012]

BIBLIOGRAPHY

U.S. Census Bureau. (2002) Section 17: Agriculture. www.census.gov/prod/2002pubs/01statab/agricult.pdf [Feb. 18, 2012]

— (2011) The 2011 Statistical Abstract: Farms—Number and Acreage by Size of Farm. USCB. www.census.gov/compendia/statab/2011/tables/11s0822.pdf [Feb. 18, 2012]

U.S. Department of Agriculture. (2007) 2007 Census of Agriculture. USDA. www.agcensus.usda.gov [Feb. 18, 2012]

— (2011) Adoption of Genetically Engineered Crops in the U.S. USDA www.ers.usda.gov/Data/BiotechCrops/ [Mar. 5, 2012]

— (2011, Feb.) Crop Values 2011 Summary. USDA. http://usda01.library.cornell.edu/usda/current/CropValuSu/CropValuSu-02-16-2012.pdf [Aug. 1, 2012]

— (2011, May) Official USDA Food Plans: Cost of Food at Home on Four Levels, U.S. Average, May 2011. USDA. www.cnpp.usda.gov/Publications/FoodPlans/2011/CostofFoodMay2011.pdf [Jul. 13, 2012]

— (n.d.) ChooseMyPlate.gov. USDA. www.choosemyplate.gov/ [Jul. 25, 2012]

Vanderlinden, Colleen. (2011, Jul.) Michigan Woman Faces 93 Days in Jail for Planting a Vegetable Garden. *Treehugger.* www.treehugger.com/greenfood/michigan-woman-faces-93-days-in-jail-for-planting-a-vegetable-garden.html [May 31, 2012]

Vidal, John. (1999, Oct.) World braced for terminator 2. *The Guardian.* www.guardian.co.uk/science/1999/oct/06/gm.food2 [Mar. 15, 2012]

Vilsack, Tom. (2010, Dec.) Open Letter to Stakeholders from Secretary Vilsack to Urge GE and non-GE Coexistence. USDA Recovery and Reinvestment Act. www.usda.gov/wps/portal/usda/!ut/p/c4/04_SB8K8xLLM9MSSzPy8xBz9CP0os_gAC9-wMJ8QY0MLF3MjA89gE28Xx0AnA2dTA_2CbEdFAD

MXUSQ!/?PC_7_P8MVVLT3104CC0ISE265GK3006005915_
navid=NEWS_RELEASE&PC_7_P8MVVLT3104CC0ISE265
GK3006005915_contentid=2010%2F12%2F0674.xml&PC_7_
P8MVVLT3104CC0ISE265GK3006005915_parentnav=LATEST_
RELEASES [May 4, 2012]

Vincent, Donovan. (2012, Aug.) Controversial dairy farmer Michael
Schmidt raided after sheep disappear. *The Star*. www.thestar.com/news/gta/
article/1238547--controversial-dairy-farmer-michael-schmidt-raided-after-
sheep-disappear [Aug. 30, 2012]

Waldie, Paul. (2010, Nov.) Canadians don't know the price of milk.
Globe and Mail. www.theglobeandmail.com/news/national/time-to-lead/
global-food/canadians-dont-know-the-price-of-milk/article1809689/
[May 16, 2012]

Waterman, Jon. (2010, Sept.) Running Dry: One Man's Journey to Raise
Awareness About the Shrinking Colorado River. Circle of Blue. www.cir-
cleofblue.org/waternews/2010/world/running-dry-one-mans-journey-to-
raise-awareness-about-the-shrinking-colorado-river/ [Apr. 17, 2012]

Wattrick, Jeff. (2011, Jun.) Despite objections from gardeners, Detroit
City Council committee recommends land sale to independent business.
MLive. www.mlive.com/news/detroit/index.ssf/2011/06/post_65.html
[Jun. 15, 2012]

Wenger, Lucia. (2011, Apr.) Who Will Feed the World? Oxfam. www.
oxfam.ca/news-and-publications/publications-and-reports/who-will-feed-
world [Jul. 13, 2012]

Whitford, David. (2009, Dec.) Can farming save Detroit? *Fortune*. http://
money.cnn.com/2009/12/29/news/economy/farming_detroit.fortune/
[Nov. 29, 2012]

BIBLIOGRAPHY

Wiedeman, Allison. (2007) USEPA CAFO Update. State CAFO Programs 2007 National CAO Roundtable. www.state-cafos.org/events/docs/WACAFO/Wiedeman.pdf

World Health Organization. (2010, May) Dioxins and their effect on human health. WHO. www.who.int/mediacentre/factsheets/fs225/en/

Wright, Karen. (2003, Aug.) Terminator Genes. *Discover Magazine.* http://discovermagazine.com/2003/aug/featgenes/ [Aug. 15, 2012]

York, Geoffrey, H. Mick. (Jul. 2008) 'Last ghost' of the Vietnam War. *The Globe and Mail.* www.theglobeandmail.com/archives/article697346.ece

Ziegler, Jean. (Jan. 2008) Report of the Special Rapporteur on the right to food. Human Rights Council, United Nations. www.righttofood.org/new/PDF/CHR2008.pdf [Jul. 11, 2012]

Index